70-2284

PR
6019
09
Z52563

Arnold
James Joyce.

JUL 2000

Date Due

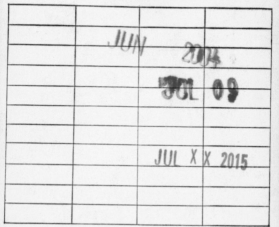

	JUN	2004	
		JUL 09	
		JUL X X 2015	

JAMES JOYCE

JAMES JOYCE

Armin Arnold

Frederick Ungar Publishing Co.
New York

70-2284

Published by special arrangement with Colloquium Verlag, Berlin, publishers of the original German *James Joyce*. Translated and completely revised by Armin Arnold with Judy Young.

Copyright © 1969 by Frederick Ungar Publishing Co., Inc.
Printed in the United States of America
Library of Congress Catalog Number: 68-31445
Standard Book Number: 8044-2007-6

Contents

1

The Martyr

The three outstanding English novelists of the first half of this century are, no doubt, Joseph Conrad, D. H. Lawrence, and James Joyce. It would be difficult to find three literary geniuses who have less in common. It is therefore not surprising that they did not feel any affection for each other's work. Lawrence considered Conrad's *Heart of Darkness* a cheap novel of adventure, and *Lord Jim* was, for him, a sentimental romance. Joyce knew Lawrence's novels *The Rainbow* and *Lady Chatterley's Lover*, and he was anything but enthusiastic about them. Lawrence, on the other hand, felt nothing but contempt and disgust for *Ulysses* and the fragments of *Finnegans Wake* which he had read in the Paris magazine *transition*. Of these three literary giants, Conrad is now an established classic writer; Lawrence's works are the most widely read and still carry the flavor of the sensational; and Joyce has had more influence on present world literature than almost any other writer.

James Joyce was born in Dublin on the second of February 1882; his family belonged to the upper-middle class. At the age of six he was sent to Clongowes Wood, a high-class boarding school run by Jesuits. He was an excellent pupil. His father, John Stanislaus Joyce, was no friend of the Church; he was a dedicated partisan of Parnell who, according to John Joyce, had been "betrayed" by the Church because he had committed adultery. In June 1891, James Joyce had to leave Clongowes Wood and went to live with his family. His father had lost his position in the government but had been granted a pension of £132. This would have been enough for him and his family, but John Joyce was addicted to an elegant way of life. Instead of adapting his expenses to his reduced income, he spent more money than ever. He sold and mortgaged the land and the buildings he owned. The Joyce family had to move into more and more shabby houses in less and less respectable parts of Dublin. For a while Joyce became a pupil at the lower-class school of the Christian Brothers. In 1893, he entered Belvedere, a Jesuit college, where, at the recommendation of the former rector of Clongowes Wood, he was exempted from paying fees. As before, he was an outstanding student and won several prizes in English composition. After 1894, the once prosperous family lived in poverty. The parents quarreled frequently, and the children on one occasion had to prevent John Joyce from strangling his wife. James Joyce got on with his father better than did his brothers and sisters; nevertheless, he must have suffered greatly from the tragic atmosphere at home. At Belvedere College and later at University College, Joyce's friends and colleagues came from the upper-middle classes, from circles in which the financial collapse of John Joyce was only too well known. Although his colleagues were tactful, James was conscious of their thoughts. It is therefore easy to understand Joyce's proud and often arrogant behavior during the following years.

C. P. Curran suggests that this arrogance might have been a product of Joyce's reading of D'Annunzio. D'Annunzio had described the artist as a

Nietzschean Zarathustra, that is, as a special kind of human being who must preserve his talents by keeping himself out of and above the "rabblement" of average human beings. He must be an honest egotist, think of himself and his art first, and feel no compassion for others. In their book *The Workshop of Daedalus*, Robert Scholes and Richard M. Kain quote several relevant passages which Joyce had read. The first is from D'Annunzio's *Le vergini delle Rocce* (transl. 1898): "The world is the representation of the sensibility and the thought of a few superior men who have made it what it is, and in the course of time broadened and adorned it. In the future they will still further amplify and enrich it, and the world as it today appears, is a magnificent gift granted by the few to the many, from the free to the slaves, from those who think and feel, to those who must work." [1] Joyce had also read Oscar Wilde's essay "The Soul of Man under Socialism" (1891):

Now and then, in the course of the century, a great man of science, like Darwin; a great poet, like Keats; a fine critical spirit like M. Renan; a supreme artist like Flaubert, has been able to isolate himself, to keep himself out of reach of the clamorous claims of others, to stand, "under the shelter of the wall," as Plato puts it, and so to realize the perfection of what was in him, to his own incomparable gain, and to the incomparable and lasting gain of the whole world. These, however, are exceptions. The majority of people spoil their lives by an unhealthy and exaggerated altruism—are forced, indeed, to spoil them. . . . [2]

But at the root of Joyce's lifelong arrogance lies the shame he feels about his family. Wilde and D'Annunzio and later Nietzsche may have been welcome as the means to motivate this pride.

Eugene Sheehy, one of his best friends during the Belvedere days, remembers Joyce as a "tall slight stripling with flashing teeth." He had "an icy look . . . [and a] mobile sensitive mouth. He was fond of throwing back his head as he walked, and his mood alternated between cold, slightly haughty, aloofness and sudden boisterous merriment. Sometimes his abrupt manner was a cloak for shyness." [3] In his student days, he made a great show of his undisturbable equanimity. It may be that the deterioration of his family was an important factor in his loss of faith, which probably occurred during his last year at Belvedere. The prevailing opinion among critics seems to be that Joyce left the Church because he, like Stephen Dedalus in *A Portrait of the Artist as a Young Man*, decided against the "spiritual" and for the "sensual" life. Of course his first sexual adventures had given him a guilty conscience and had made confession difficult, but most of his colleagues would have gone through the same experiences without dreaming of leaving the Church. It might well have been like this: The good Lord had not done well by the Joyces, and, like their father, James and his brother Stanislaus took their revenge by leaving the flock. In 1904 he wrote his future wife that he had left the Church "on account of the impulses of my nature." The phoniness and bad logic of the following sentences in the same letter, however, reveal at once how questionable this statement is: "I made secret war upon it [the

Church] when I was a student and declined to accept the positions it offered me. By doing this I made myself a beggar but I retained my pride. Now I make open war upon it by what I write and say and do." [4] When speaking of the Church, Joyce always used the most offensive language of which he was capable. In his letters he cursed priests, the Pope, and everything clerical in the strongest terms, and he refused to have his children baptized. About his son Giorgio, he wrote his brother Stanislaus, another Church hater: "Thanks be to the Lord Jaysus no gospeller has put his dirty face within the bawl of an ass of him [Giorgio] yet" (October 16, 1905).[5] But Joyce had every reason to be grateful to the Church, which had given him an excellent free education and had never asked anything in return. It is, however, in the nature of a man whose pride is born of feelings of inferiority to lash out against the human beings and institutions to which he owes a debt of gratitude.

From 1898 until 1902, Joyce studied at University College, but he was no longer an outstanding student. His interest turned more and more to literature. He was one of the first in Ireland to discover Ibsen. Joyce delivered a much-debated lecture on Ibsen, an attack on an earlier speech by Arthur Clery, who had compared Greek drama with the plays of the naturalists—much to the disadvantage of the latter. Joyce glorified Ibsen and rejected the Greeks (and Shakespeare) as not being adequate to the needs of modern times. More than once his modern European outlook brought him into conflict

with the majority of his colleagues who were nationalistic and whose sympathies rested with the
Irish Revival. Joyce also wrote a long review of
Ibsen's drama *When We Dead Awaken* and had the
good fortune of having it accepted by the editor of
the distinguished London *Fortnightly Review*. Ibsen read the article and sent his thanks to the un-
known author by way of his translator, William
Archer. On the occasion of Ibsen's seventy-third
anniversary, Joyce wrote a letter to the Norwegian
dramatist in which he stated that Ibsen had, indeed,
opened the way into the future, but that others,
meaning Joyce himself, would go further and produce even better works: "You have only opened the
way—though you have gone as far as you could
upon it—to the end of 'John Gabriel Borkman' and
its spiritual truth—but your last play stands, I take it,
apart. But I am sure that higher and holier enlight-
enment lies—onward." [6] Joyce received twelve
guineas for his article. One pound of this he gave to
his mother. The rest was used for a trip to London,
which he undertook in the company of his father.

Since Joyce was also interested in Gerhart
Hauptmann, he began to learn German. He translated *Michael Kramer* and parts of *Vor Sonnenauf-
gang* in the hope that Lady Gregory's new stage
would produce one of these plays. He also wrote an
original play, *A Brilliant Career*, which smacks of
Ibsen (a physician who betrays love in favor of success). William Archer read the immature product
and advised Joyce to look for another topic. The
manuscripts of this play and of a verse drama (en-

titled *Dream Stuff*) were probably burned by Joyce in 1902. His hopes that the Hauptmann would be performed came to nothing. The Irish Literary Theatre was more interested in Irish plays. Joyce attacked this attitude in his essay "The Day of the Rabblement," which should have appeared in *St. Stephen's*, the college magazine. It was not accepted, and Joyce published it, together with another rejected essay by his friend Francis Skeffington, in a pamphlet entitled *Two Essays* (1901).

About 1900, Joyce began to write a kind of prose fragment which he called "epiphanies." By the term "epiphany" he meant "a sudden, spiritual manifestation, whether in the vulgarity of speech or of gesture or in a memorable phase of the mind itself." This definition is given by Stephen Daedalus in *Stephen Hero*, the first version of *A Portrait*. Joyce gives an example of such an "epiphany." It is, in fact, merely a fragment of a conversation, jotted down in the naturalistic manner, as had been done before by Arno Holz in stories such as "Ein Tod." Stephen overhears the following syllables from the conversation of a pair of lovers in the street:

The Young Lady—(drawling discreetly) . . . O, yes . . . I was . . . at the . . . cha . . . pel. . . .

The Young Gentleman—(inaudibly) . . . I . . . (again inaudibly) . . . I . . .

The Young Lady—(softly) . . . O . . . but you're . . . ve . . . ry . . . wick . . . ed. . . .

Like Joyce, Stephen thought of collecting and publishing a book of epiphanies: "He believed that it was for the man of letters to record these epiphanies with extreme care, seeing that they themselves are the most delicate and evanescent of moments." [7] It seems that by 1902 Joyce had a good collection of epiphanies which he showed to his friends with pride. In *As I Was Going down Sackville Street* (1937), Oliver St. John Gogarty makes fun of Joyce's habit of slipping away to the lavatory to write down fragments of the conversation. He calls an epiphany a "showing forth of the mind by which he [Joyce] considered one gave oneself away." [8]

In 1956, O. A. Silverman published twenty-two such epiphanies which had found their way into the Lockwood Memorial Library in Buffalo. Nine years later, Robert Scholes and Richard M. Kain collected all the forty extant epiphanies in *The Workshop of Daedalus*. In part, they are short dialogues which Joyce heard in the street and which he felt had a strange suggestive power. In part, they are descriptions, combinations of words, images, and analogies which Joyce had spontaneously put to paper as they occurred to him. Here is an example of the second kind:

A white mist is falling in slow flakes. The path leads me down to an obscure pool. Something is moving in the pool; it is an arctic beast with a rough yellow coat. I thrust in my stick and as he rises out of the water I see that his back slopes towards the croup and that he is very sluggish. I am not afraid but, thrusting at him often with my stick drive him before me. He moves his paws heavily and mutters words of some language which I do not understand. [9]

Joyce made use of these epiphanies again and again, first in *Stephen Hero* and then in several of his later works. It is interesting to note here that one of Joyce's favorite authors, Gerhart Hauptmann, had collected such epiphanies in the 1880s when, as a young man, he walked through the streets with a notebook and a pencil in his hand attempting to catch and preserve such spoken fragments of "life."

John Joyce hoped his son would take on a well-paid position at the Guinness brewery and support the family. James Joyce, however, decided to enter St. Cecilia Medical School and become a doctor. Meanwhile his father had sold the rights to half his pension and bought a house. The five and a half pounds a week which he had left were insufficient, and John Joyce began taking up one mortgage after another until, in 1905, he had to sell the house and begin paying rent again—on half his previous income. Joyce (whose talents lay elsewhere) had difficulties with science courses, and he could not pay the fees. The university would not support him by giving him a tutorship. Joyce now felt, rightly or wrongly, that Ireland had rejected him and decided to leave the country. Acting and feeling as a martyr —a pose which he enjoyed and tried to keep up for the rest of his life—he went into voluntary exile in Paris in 1902. He had the intention of studying medicine at the Sorbonne, but there was little reason to suppose that he would succeed in Paris after he had failed in Dublin. In any case, he did not take his plans to study medicine too seriously, since he wanted to become a writer. As C. P. Curran says, Joyce *had* to leave; if he had stayed, he would have had to work and support the family or, what is more probable, he would have followed in his father's footsteps. If he had gone to London, nobody would have thought of him as an "exile"—many young men with literary ambitions went to London. Shaw, Wilde, and Yeats certainly did not consider themselves exiles. But in Paris or even Trieste—this was altogether different. Richard Ellmann says: "Joyce needed exile as a reproach to others and a justification of himself." [10] Like other revolutionaries, Joyce "fattened on opposition and grew thin and pale when treated with indulgence. Whenever his relations with his native land were in danger of improving, he was to find a new incident to solidify his intransigence and to reaffirm the rightness of his voluntary absence." [11]

In spite of his moderate enthusiasm for the "cause," Joyce had connections with some of the leaders of the Irish cultural renaissance in Dublin; among these were Lady Gregory, William Butler Yeats, and George Russell (known under the pseudonym AE). Russell and Yeats thought highly of him, and both were often to be of help to him. When Joyce was on his way to Paris, Yeats put him up in London and introduced him to Arthur Symons, an influential critic who later took great pains to find him a publisher. Lady Gregory was also helpful by arranging for him to review books for the Dublin *Daily Express*. During his first year in Paris, Joyce reviewed about twenty books. These reviews, together with some lectures and other critical essays, were collected by Ellsworth Mason and Richard Ellmann in 1959 (*The Critical Writings of James Joyce*).

Joyce's first stay in Paris was not long. He did not understand the lectures at the Sorbonne, had no money, and could not find enough pupils who were interested in taking private lessons in English. He felt ill and homesick. His kindhearted father took out another mortgage and sent him the money for the return journey. Two days before Christmas, after a three-week absence, Joyce was back in Dublin. But a month later he left again; his sense of honor would not allow him to stay at home. He had decided to be a martyr and an exile, and nothing in the world would have made him give up this role. In Paris, he made his living mainly by giving a few private lessons, by borrowing money, and by asking for help from his parents. He rarely had any luck with newspaper editors, and only the columns of the *Daily Express* remained open to him. (In 1903, he also published a review in the London *Speaker* and an interview piece in the *Irish Times*.) He regularly wrote to his mother describing how he was starving and freezing, whereupon the good woman would pawn something in order to send him a few shillings. John Synge was another Irishman who tried—unsuccessfully—to establish himself in Paris; Joyce met him and was one of the first to read the manuscript of the play which was later to become famous, *Riders to the Sea*. At that time Joyce pretended not to think much of it but later changed his mind and translated it into Italian. He was by no means idle. He wrote several poems for a volume which he intended to call "Book of Songs," a title inspired by Heinrich Heine. He must have come across Heine when preparing a paper on J. C. Mangan, who had translated Heine into English and was himself influenced by the German poet. Joyce may have been aware that his poems had the same quality as Heine's: they could easily be put to music. He also wrote epiphanies and read considerably in the Paris libraries. On a trip to Tours, he picked up Edouard Dujardin's novel *Les Lauriers sont coupés*, from which, as he himself said, he learned the technique of the interior monologue, which he was to use in *Ulysses*. On April 10, 1904, he received a telegram saying his mother was dying. Joyce borrowed some money from one of his pupils and traveled back to Ireland the next day. He was to remain in Dublin for a year and a half.

During this stay Joyce came under the influence of Oliver Gogarty, who was his superior in wit and intellect. He encouraged Joyce to drink, and Joyce indulged in this passion for the rest of his life, bringing unhappiness on himself and his family. His mother, who was suffering from an incurable cancer, was very religious, and it grieved her that Joyce would not go to Easter communion. From about this time on, his younger brother, Stanislaus, who had always admired him greatly, became his most faithful friend. He later followed Joyce into "exile" and only dissociated himself from his brother after the First World War. In contrast to Joyce, Stanislaus was modest and had little humor; he did not drink, and he hated his father who was constantly drunk. Stanislaus kept a diary which James read and ridiculed. Fundamentally, he despised his younger brother and exploited him quite ruthlessly. Joyce's elder friends also made fun of the earnest and faithful Stanislaus, and one of them, Vincent Cosgrave, called him James' ape.

The Irish were not yet prepared to take Joyce's "greatness" seriously, for what he had produced up to that time was not worth the bother. But Joyce demanded to be treated as though he had already written several masterpieces. All the same, wherever he knocked the doors were opened to him, and his martyrdom was his own invention. The so-called exile forced on him was, in fact, a product of his fantasy and served him as an excuse for—and a justification of—both his mismanaged life and the frequently cruel treatment of his former friends. His mother died on August 13, 1903, at the age of only forty-four. Joyce did not think of going back to Paris at the moment. He tried in vain to obtain a position in the National Library. Then Skeffington suggested that he teach four evening lessons in French, but Joyce declined—he did not want to have to be grateful to anybody at his old university. He tried medical school again but not for long. A project to start a newspaper came to nothing when the necessary capital could not be procured. Finally, Joyce even succeeded in quarreling with the editor of the *Daily Express* and so lost his last source of income.

Living at home was anything but pleasant. After his mother's death, the household consisted of the father, three sons, one aunt, and six sisters. Two of the brothers drank heavily, and none of them contributed to the household expenses. The girls, of course, were not permitted to work except at home. John Joyce had mortgaged everything possible by now. James taught for a few weeks at a private school in Dalkey (an experience used in the second chapter of *Ulysses*); he was enlarging into a novel a sketch that had been offered to and refused by a periodical. This was to be *Stephen Hero*, a largely satirical and almost completely autobiographical novel which he later remodeled into *A Portrait*. It was originally more than 900 pages long; the 383 pages which were preserved were published posthumously in 1944; they correspond, so far as the contents are concerned, to the last third of *A Portrait*. New editions include some additional pages found later. Although Joyce rejected *Stephen Hero* as being the product of a schoolboy, the fragment is very readable. The novel lacks form, and the main character is a tremendous bore, a kind of juvenile Zarathustra. Stephen (James Joyce) is the brilliant hero, the freedom fighter, the artist who breaks through the barriers of bourgeois tradition, tears away the deceiving mask from the Catholic Church, and sacrifices prosperity for truth in art. His friends and colleagues, on the other hand, are mostly stupid, mean, and evil; they are Judases who are striving to betray Stephen, the Christ.

The hero's name is Stephen Daedalus. "Stephen" stands for the Christian martyr of that name, and "Daedalus" stands for the greatest inventor of antiquity. Joyce was being stoned like Stephen, but like Daedalus, he would escape from the island on which he was a captive. The title, *Stephen Hero*, points out that Joyce was not without self-criticism; he protected himself by an ironic title. The strength of the book lies in the dialogue passages, which are always good and often witty. The characters come to life in their manner of speaking. The fragment is about the death of Stephen's sister (excellently described), Stephen's unhappy love affair with Emma, his relationship to his parents and his friends, life in Dublin in general, and about art. Stephen has lost his faith, and the scene in which he admits this to his mother is probably the most memorable one in the book. Stephen may be an arrogant and conceited bore, but he has some refreshing qualities: he can think logically, and he can be extremely honest, as when he tells the conventional Emma that he would like to spend the night with her and then not see her again. He recognizes phoniness at once—people only pretend to be sad after his sister's death. Stephen is, of course, largely a phony himself. He is the person who, on paper behaved as James Joyce himself wished he had behaved.

The book provides valuable insight into the biography and psychology of the young Joyce. Even here, Joyce voices the opinion that words are too carelessly used. Stephen reads Skeat's *Etymological Dictionary* with avid interest. This preoccupation with words (and their abuse) eventually leads Joyce to *Finnegans Wake*. Joyce also believed, as did Stephen, that all art must be autobiographical, for it is the writer who is at the center of life; he is the one who can completely absorb the life around him and give it general validity by transforming it into art. In the summer of 1904 a large part of the novel was finished, and Joyce gave the manuscript to several friends to read. In addition to the novel, Joyce wrote poetry, and he also found time for drinking and visiting brothels. Like his father, Joyce had an outstanding tenor voice, and it is probable that he could have had a successful musical career. In 1904 he took part in a singing contest which he would have won had he also been able to sing directly from a musical score. As it was, he had to be satisfied with the bronze medal.

On June 10, 1904, Joyce met his future wife, Nora Barnacle, the daughter of a Galway baker; she was working in a Dublin hotel at that time. They had their first date on June 16, and it was this day which Joyce later chose as the date of his eighteen-hour novel, *Ulysses*. He fell head over heels in love with the pretty but intellectually unpretentious girl. When, in the autumn, Joyce left Ireland for good, Nora went with him. In many respects she resembled Heinrich Heine's wife, a fact which Joyce noted in a letter to his brother Stanislaus (January 19, 1905). Like Mathilde, Nora could barely read and write and had no understanding of the artistic achievements of her husband; she hated to write letters; she was just as pretty and just as devoted. In both cases, it was a continuing passionate and sexually fulfilling relationship. Heine and Joyce married late in life and both for testamentary reasons.

Joyce had shown *Stephen Hero* to George Russell. Russell suggested that Joyce write some simple stories for the periodical *Irish Homestead*; he would be well paid, and he could publish under a pseudonym if he wanted to. Joyce needed the money and wrote several stories under the pen name S. D. (Stephen Dedalus); three of these were published in August, September, and December 1904. Joyce's collection of short stories, *Dubliners*, grew out of these tales. During the summer and autumn of 1904, Joyce lived mostly away from home—with friends. In September he spent a week with Gogarty in the Martello Tower at Sandycove. It is the scene of the first chapter of *Ulysses* and has become a famous place of pilgrimage for Joyceans. Gogarty had rented the miniature fortress for a year from the Secretary of State for War. But Joyce and Gogarty did not get along, and Joyce was evicted. He was never to forgive Gogarty for this. He now definitely made up his mind to leave Ireland and take Nora with him. He paid two guineas to an agent who pretended she had secured a position for him at the Berlitz school in Zurich. With great difficulties Joyce borrowed enough money to get Nora and himself started on the trip. Stanislaus seems to have been the only one in the family who knew about the existence of Nora; John Joyce found out only after the young pair had left.

2

Into Exile

James Joyce and Nora Barnacle arrived in London on October 9, 1904. The following day they were in Paris and on the eleventh in Zurich. The Berlitz school knew nothing of Joyce and had no vacancy. The director sent Joyce to Trieste, from where he was sent on to Pola (today a town in Yugoslavia) where a new Berlitz school was about to be opened. Pola was, at that time, a lively naval base within the Austrian Empire, and many pupils of the Berlitz school were naval officers. Joyce received £2 a week for sixteen hours instruction. He was able to buy a new suit and have his teeth fixed. He continued to work on *Stephen Hero*, wrote an occasional short story or poem, and managed to read considerably, wearing a pince-nez with strong glasses. In March 1905, a spy ring was discovered in Pola, and all foreigners were asked to leave. Joyce was lucky and got a position at the Berlitz school in Trieste.

The child Nora had been expecting was born in Trieste on July 27, 1905; the child, a son, was named George (Giorgio). Nora suffered from depressions during her pregnancy, and Joyce started drinking again. He stayed out until late at night, and his debts grew continuously. However, he found enough time to finish twelve stories of *Dubliners* and sent them to the publisher, Grant Richards, who already had the manuscript of a small book of poetry, *Chamber Music*. When a second position for English became vacant at the Berlitz school in Trieste, Joyce wrote to his brother, Stanislaus, who arrived in Trieste at the end of October 1905.

Stanislaus realized soon enough that he had been given a bad deal. His brother and his sister-in-law used him as much as they could. His salary went directly into the pocket of James who invested it in drink. Stanislaus spent most of his time trying to console Nora and searching the bars for his brother to drag him home. As only one teacher was needed in the summer of 1906, James decided to accept a well-paid position as a correspondent in a bank in Rome. Stanislaus stayed behind and gradually paid back part of his brother's debts. Although he earned twice as much as in Trieste, Joyce was still unable to make ends meet. He borrowed right and left, even at the English consulate. What money Stanislaus did not use to appease the creditors in Trieste, he had to send on to Rome.

Chamber Music was turned down by Grant Richards but was accepted by Elkin Mathews on the recommendation of Arthur Symons. The little book was published in 1907. The best edition is that of William York Tindall (New York, 1954), which is provided with an extensive critical apparatus. The poems are short, readable pieces, faultless in form, and are well suited to be lyrics for songs. In fact, they have often been set to music. Few critics, however, are convinced that Joyce was a great lyric poet. His themes and his choice of words and rhymes are conventional; it is, fundamentally, the usual love and dream stuff produced by young poets at the turn of the century. Joyce himself was by no means enthusiastic about his achievement. He wrote to his brother on October 18, 1906: "I went

through my entire book of verses mentally on re-
ceipt of Symons' letter and they nearly all seemed to
me poor and trivial: some phrases and lines pleased
me and no more. A page of 'A Little Cloud' [a short
story] gives me more pleasure than all my verses." [1]
After he had corrected the page proofs in April
1907, he even wanted to stop the publication of the
book. "All that kind of thing is false," he said to
Stanislaus. [2]

Joyce had no luck with *Dubliners*. It took him
nine years to convince a publisher and a printer to
accept these—as they seem to us today—harmless,
naturalistic sketches. Grant Richards was at first
willing to publish them. Soon, however, warned by
the printer, he grew apprehensive and wanted to
have a story left out and several passages in others
changed. Richards had just been through a bank-
ruptcy and could not afford any trouble. He had to
be apprehensive about the censor and the lawsuits
which might be brought against him by those Dubliners whom Joyce, often without changing their
names, had used in the stories. Place names are generally unchanged, too (those of public houses, for
instance). Over and above this, Joyce had used
"forbidden" words such as "bloody," and King Edward VII was mentioned in a rather unflattering
way: "He's just an ordinary knockabout like you
and me. He's fond of his glass of grog and he's a bit
of a rake, perhaps, and he's a good sportsman." [3]
After Grant Richards, the book was considered and
rejected by John Long; finally Maunsel & Co. in
Dublin accepted the manuscript and had it printed.

Then the director, George Roberts, suddenly pan-
icked; it had struck him that he might be sued. He
refused to distribute the books, and the printer had
them pulped.

At first there were only twelve stories. In 1914,
the year of publication, three more were added,
among these the longest and best, "The Dead."
Dubliners is the best introduction to Joyce. The
main theme and various characters of the later
works can already be found here. The form, however, is still conventional, and the book can be understood without reference to scholarly interpretations. There are no dramatically sharpened plots, no
unexpected culminating or turning points; the stories
are, in fact, prolonged epiphanies, scenes, or
sketches which may be interpreted symbolically despite the fact that they are written in a traditional,
naturalistic style. In this respect, they have much in
common with the sketches in Arno Holz and Jo-
hannes Schlaf's *Papa Hamlet* (1889).

In *A Reader's Guide to James Joyce*, William
York Tindall has tried to interpret *Dubliners* symbolically. Joyce's main concern, he says, was to depict Dublin as a town full of the intellectually lame
and crippled. People are impotent, they are not successful, and they are disappointed. This is shown on
three different levels: moral, intellectual, and spiritual. The climax of some stories is the moment
when a protagonist suddenly becomes aware of his
situation and for the first time perceives the truth
about himself. The last of the stories, "The Dead"
(written in 1907), may serve as an example of this.

Gabriel Conroy and his wife go to a social gathering given every year by two of his aunts. Every year the food is the same, the conversation is the same, and the whole procedure is the same. The description of the guests—people who are not even aware that they are wearing masks—could be by Chekhov. Conroy and his wife go to a hotel afterwards. Gabriel is full of tenderness and love, but on this evening he hears, for the first time in all his years of marriage, that he was not the first man in his wife's life. A seventeen-year-old youth who suffered from tuberculosis had loved her and, despite his illness, had come to her window at night when he had heard that she was leaving for a boarding school. He died of the cold which he caught on this occasion and so had given his life for her. This bit of information is Gabriel's epiphany. His sexual impulses disappear for the moment; the image that he has had of his wife is destroyed. Outwardly, there is not much action; it all takes place inside Gabriel. The story, as almost everything Joyce wrote, has autobiographical roots; Nora had had such a love affair in Galway. The long description of the party has little to do with the final epiphany, but Joyce felt he had omitted one good Irish quality in the fourteen previous stories: the people's hospitality. In Chapter 15 of his Joyce biography, Richard Ellmann analyzes all the autobiographical and literary sources of the story and how Joyce had made use of them. These fourteen pages are an excellent introduction into Joyce's "workshop," into his way of thinking, combining, and constructing.

The first three stories of *Dubliners* are told in the first person. On page one, the boy, who tells the story, ponders the word "paralysis." This is not by accident. In a letter to Grant Richards dated May 5, 1906, Joyce wrote: "My intention was to write a chapter of the moral history of my country and I chose Dublin for the scene because that city seemed to me the centre of paralysis." [4] Most stories show the spiritual paralysis in the life of Dubliners. As in *Stephen Hero*, the dialogue is the best part. The stories as a whole are a kind of miniature *La Comédie humaine*. Each story shows at least one aspect of Dublin life and introduces one or several different characters. In the first three stories we meet the boy's aunt and uncle and the atmosphere of their hollow lives. In the fourth we meet a girl who cannot find the courage to leave Ireland with her lover, and in the next one Joyce tries to depict the upper crust of society. In "Two Gallants" a gentleman extracts money from a girl, and in "The Boarding House" a ruthless mother forces a harmless and cowardly young man with a steady income to marry her daughter. In "A Little Cloud" Joyce contrasts a loud-mouthed emigrant with a modest family man, and the latter becomes aware of his hopeless situation as a prisoner on the island. "Counterparts" describes the life of an office employee who suffers through the day in order to be able to join his friends in the pub in the evening; his hatred of his employer is transformed to hatred of his children when he finally comes home. In "Clay" Joyce describes a woman destined never to know the happiness of love or travel. In "A Painful Case" a blood-less puritan has the good fortune to be loved by an excellent woman; however, he is incapable of phys-ical affection, and the woman ends her life under a train. "Ivy Day in the Committee Room" is polit-ical, "Grace" religious, and "A Mother" psycholog-ical satire. *Dubliners* is, in a sense, a justification for Joyce's exile. The book shows what he would have become had he stayed in his native city.

Joyce had, as in the case of *Chamber Music*, some doubts about the quality of his stories. In a letter to Stanislaus, written on July 19, 1905, he meditated:

The stories in *Dubliners* seem to be indisputably well done but, after all, perhaps many people could do them as well. I am not rewarded by any feeling of having overcome diffi-culties. Maupassant writes very well, of course, but I am afraid that his moral sense is rather obtuse. The Dublin papers will object to my stories as to a caricature of Dublin life. Do you think there is any truth in this? At times the spirit directing my pen seems to me so plainly mischievous that I am almost prepared to let the Dublin critics have their way.[5]

Joyce's worries about the critics' reactions were premature; the book did not come out until nine years later.

Throughout his life, Joyce took pains to foster his aversion to the Ireland which had betrayed him and to keep the wound open deliberately. The feel-ing of being a martyr was a prerequisite and the main inspiration for his artistic creativity. He had the gift of making his life difficult and of getting into trouble quite unnecessarily. Particularly from the financial point of view, he was quite irresponsible. In March 1907, Joyce gave up his lucrative position in Rome in order to return to Trieste, although Stanislaus had written to him that there were not enough pupils in Trieste for two teachers. His last night in Rome was spent in drinking, and he was robbed of his whole month's salary. Nora was again expecting a child. Probably the real reason for wanting to get away was the fact that he had written very little in Rome. In March 1907, he wrote to Stanislaus: "I have come to the conclusion that it is about time I made up my mind whether I am to become a writer. . . . I foresee that I shall have to do other work as well but to continue as I am at present would certainly mean my mental extinction. It is months since I have written a line. . . ." [6] His salary was good, but he had to work for it from eight-thirty in the morning to seven-thirty at night. The rest of his time was spent dining out, going to the theater, and reading in a café. Nevertheless, it was in Rome that the original idea of *Ulysses* was born. He planned to write a story about a Dublin Jew, Mr. Alfred H. Hunter, who was said to have an unfaithful wife.

Joyce was given six hours of teaching a week at the Trieste Berlitz school. A friend and student of his commissioned some articles for his newspaper, *Il Piccolo della Sera*. Joyce wrote three in 1907 (all on politics in Ireland), two in 1909 (on Wilde and Shaw), one on home rule in 1910, and three more on Irish affairs in 1912. Another student suggested that he give three public lectures on Ireland at the Uni-

versità del Popolo. Joyce was glad to oblige and lec-
tured on Irish history, on James Clarence Mangan,
and on the Irish literary renaissance. All this
brought in little money. In addition, the Joyce
family in Dublin was hard up, and James had to send
an occasional pound to his father.

In July and August, Joyce spent a few weeks
in the hospital with rheumatic fever, which—he
thought—was a result of the nights he had slept in
the gutter. Meanwhile, Stanislaus was looking after
the family and had to borrow money again. Lucia
Anna was born in the pauper ward on July 26,
1907; she was to become his main worry in the last
years of his life. His eyes grew suddenly very much
worse; in May 1908, he had a bad attack of iritis and
had to give up drinking for a few months. In the
next two decades operation followed operation, and
the best known pictures of Joyce show him with a
black patch over one eye or wearing dark glasses.
The only pleasing events in the life of the family
were Stanislaus' appointment as acting director of
the Berlitz school and the friendship between Joyce
and Ettore Schmitz, a businessman who was taught
English by Joyce and who, under the pseudonym of
Italo Svevo, became one of the best known Italian
writers of this century. In spite of all, Joyce continued to write. He finished "The Dead" (and with
this story the final version of *Dubliners*), and he
began to rewrite *Stephen Hero* in a shorter five-part
version. By April 1908, he had completed the first
three chapters.

In July 1909, Joyce borrowed money and went
to Ireland with his small son, Giorgio. He took plea-

sure in showing his former friends and colleagues that he was not to be reconciled. But they took their revenge. One of them, Cosgrave, told Joyce that Nora had gone out with him at the same time that she had gone out with Joyce. Whenever she had told Joyce that she had to work late at the hotel, she had, in fact, spent the evening with Cosgrave. On hearing this, Joyce broke down for two days, until a better friend, John Francis Byrne, pointed out to him that Cosgrave had lied. The letters which Joyce wrote to Nora at the time are among his most moving ones; they show how much his peace of mind depended on her. Joyce had to wait in Dublin until Stanislaus could scratch enough money together to pay for the return trip. On September 9, he went back to Italy with his sister Eva, who was to look after the household in Trieste. Another sister went to New Zealand as a nun, so that John Joyce was left with only four daughters.

A month later Joyce was back in Dublin, this time to open a cinema. He had convinced some businessmen who ran two cinemas in Trieste and one in Bucharest that they could make profits in Dublin as well. Joyce's fare was paid; he received a living allowance, and he was to get ten per cent of the profits. On December 20, Joyce opened the Volta cinema, the first film theater in Dublin. It was lucky for his Dublin relations that he happened to be there because his father was in the hospital, and the four daughters had to be provided for. One of the Trieste partners took over the administration of the cinema, and Joyce traveled back to Italy on January 2, 1910; this time he took his sister Eileen with him.

The household in Trieste now consisted of two sisters, two brothers, Nora, and her two children. The sisters, of course, only increased the financial problems. It was Stanislaus who was the main provider for everybody, although Joyce still gave private lessons in the afternoon. In the evenings, he would eat out and go to the theater, or he would get rid of what he had earned during the day in a tavern. By the summer of 1911, Eva had had enough of the chaotic situation and went back to Ireland. Shortly after her return, Joyce's sister Mabel died of typhoid fever. The Volta cinema did not pay and had to be sold at a loss.

While negotiations about *Dubliners* continued, Joyce was preparing two lectures, one on Daniel Defoe and the other on William Blake, which he delivered at the Università Popolare in March 1912. In April, with great success, he passed examinations at the University of Padua to obtain a teacher's certificate in Italian and English. However, he was finally refused a diploma because his Dublin bachelor of arts degree was not considered equivalent to Italian prerequisites for the diploma. In early July, Nora and Lucia traveled to Ireland to spend a few weeks in Galway with Nora's relatives. Since Joyce did not receive a letter within a week, he became frightened, borrowed money from Italo Svevo, and followed her, taking Giorgio with him. Eileen, who stayed behind, had no money and was evicted from the apartment. As always, Stanislaus had to take care of the situation. Meanwhile Joyce tried to get George Roberts at Maunsel & Co. to publish *Dub-*

liners. He made almost every concession asked for; he agreed to deletions and changes of names and places. It was quite apparent that Roberts did not want to bring out the book, but, the agreement having been signed, he did not want to say so outright. He also must have had a grudge against Joyce, who had published a letter in *Sinn Fein*, in which he had enumerated the difficulties he had encountered with *Dubliners*, mentioning Grant Richards and Maunsel & Co. by name. Although the printing had only cost £60, Roberts now asked for securities of £1000 in case he should be prosecuted. He knew well enough that Joyce was penniless. Next, he said that Joyce had broken the contract by submitting a libelous book and asked him to pay part of the publisher's expenses. Roberts then proposed that Joyce buy the printed sheets for £30; but before such a deal could be concluded, the printer, on September 11, destroyed the sheets. Joyce left Ireland on the same day, never to return. Each time he had visited Dublin he had run into trouble and bad luck. He was convinced that, should he come a fourth time, he would suffer bodily harm. Back in Trieste, he printed a broadside against Roberts, "Gas from a Burner," which he sent to his brother Charles in Dublin, who distributed it among friends and enemies.

Joyce's financial situation improved at the Scuola Revoltella Superiore di Commercio, where he taught English in the mornings. In the afternoon he received private pupils, with one of whom—Amalia Popper, a Jewish girl of about seventeen—he fell in love. In his biography of Joyce, Richard Ellmann states that Joyce wrote "an account of the affair in his best calligraphy under the ironic title of *Giacomo* [Casanova] *Joyce*." [7] He then proceeds to quote most of the account—about two pages of small print. Nine years later (by 1968), Ellmann had made up his mind that the manuscript was, in fact, an unpublished masterpiece and deserved to be edited in a separate book. The manuscript is said to represent Joyce's "discovery of a new form of imaginative expression." [8] *Giacomo Joyce* "stands now in its own terms as a great achievement. To readers accustomed by Joyce to large formal structures, the size and informality of this most delicate of novels [sic!] may be especially ingratiating." [9] Joyce had written the material on sixteen pages, leaving large spaces between paragraphs (which sometimes consist of only one short sentence). He had once produced a manuscript copy of *Chamber Music* as a present for Nora. *Giacomo Joyce* may have been intended as a present to Amalia, but her cool attitude toward him would have discouraged him from presenting her with the manuscript. (She must have had some respect for him as an author, since she translated five stories from *Dubliners* into Italian. [Trieste, 1935]). Evidently the large empty spaces between the paragraphs are there for the sake of calligraphic beauty—and to extend the material from four to sixteen pages. It seems improbable that Joyce ever thought of publishing this manuscript. But he did make use of it, treating the paragraphs as epiphanies and using them when writing *A Portrait*

of the Artist as a Young Man, Exiles, and *Ulysses.*
The contents: Joyce describes the girl, his feelings
toward her, dreams and visions he has of her, an
encounter with her father, her behavior toward
him, and his ironic resignation at the end. Even some
of the most faithful Joyceans hesitated at the word
"novel" and preferred to call the product a cycle of
prose poems. This is much more to the point: as
usual, Joyce avoids any kind of cliché, and the paragraphs read like a series of epiphanies—or rather
like a series of notes which could later serve as skeleton pieces for a short story or a short novel.

In November 1913, Joyce gave ten lectures on
Hamlet at the Università del Popolo. *Dubliners*
went to Martin Secker and Elkin Mathews and was
rejected by both. Then he received a letter from
Grant Richards who said he wanted to consider
Dubliners again. In addition, Ezra Pound wrote
from London that he wanted to include Joyce's
poem "I Hear an Army" in the first Imagist anthol-
ogy. He also offered his help in getting Joyce's
other works published. Yeats had told Pound about
Joyce, who now sent him his poems, the entire manuscript of *Dubliners,* and the first chapter of *A Portrait.* Pound arranged the publication of *A Portrait*
as a serial in *The Egoist.* Dora Marsden was the editor, soon to be followed by Harriet Weaver. The
latter gave Joyce backing and support for the rest
of his life.

Pound, who had an extraordinary talent for or-
ganization and propaganda, set things going. On
January 15, 1914, he published a report about

Joyce's difficulties with *Dubliners*. Two weeks later, Grant Richards accepted the manuscript for publication. The contract was anything but favorable: Joyce received no royalties for the first 500 copies and had to commit himself to buying 120 copies himself. *Dubliners* appeared on June 15, 1914, and had no trouble with the censors. It sold badly, about 250 copies during the first year. The first installment of *A Portrait* appeared on February 2, 1914; the final chapter was finished in the summer of 1915.

A *Portrait* is the story of a young man growing up, an Irish *Wilhelm Meister*. Critics always point out that Stephen Dedalus should not be identified with Joyce because, after all, he is a fictitious character. On the other hand, there is no doubt that almost everything that Stephen experiences had also been experienced by Joyce. A simultaneous reading of *A Portrait* and the corresponding chapters in Richard Ellmann's biography makes this quite clear. What is the novel all about? One could say that *A Portrait* consists of a series of epiphanies—descriptive sketches and dialogues—which have more unity than *Dubliners* because the personnel is more limited. Joyce, like Proust, is a master of memory, not so much in visualizing pictures as in remembering dialogues. The strength of the book is its dialogue; the speeches sound as real as if Joyce had carried a tape recorder with him. The novel could thus be compared not to a film but to a lecture with slides in which a colored but static picture is projected as a background while a reporter with a phenomenal memory reproduces the conversations which took place at the time the picture was taken.

Dubliners is, in a way, Joyce's justification for his exile. In *A Portrait* he tries to show why he left the Church. Every scene in every chapter contributes another reason. In the Christmas scene, his father and Mr. Casey—the boy's sympathies are with them, not with the women—take the part of Parnell and accuse the Church of hypocrisy. Shortly afterwards, Stephen experiences the injustice of the Church himself. He has broken his glasses. Father Dolan, representing the Church, believes that Stephen has done so intentionally in order to be excused from class work, and Stephen is caned. He takes his revenge by complaining to the rector. The rector seems to help him, but his behavior is hypocritical: he tells Father Dolan about Stephen's complaint, and the two priests have a good laugh about the boy's injured sense of justice. In Chapter 1, the seeds of his later hatred for the Church are sown in Stephen's subconscious mind.

In Chapter 2, Stephen is in another Jesuit college, Belvedere. Again, he comes into conflict with the authorities. His pride is hurt when he has to recant an apparently heretical statement. He is now sixteen years old, and he has preserved his sense of justice, his idealism. He cannot compromise, he hates hypocrisy. He cannot sin, confess with tears in his eyes, and then go and sin again—an attitude which his colleagues (and the Church) seem to accept as quite natural. We can therefore imagine the conflict in Stephen's soul after he has visited a brothel and committed a mortal sin. If he does not regret the sin, then his cofession would be phony. Either he can really regret, confess, and make up his mind never to commit this sin again, or he should in all honesty leave the Church whose commandments he cannot obey.

The best means for the Church to wake up the conscience of hardened sinners is a retreat, especially if it is preached by Jesuits. The technique of the priest in charge of the retreat is this: hell, the punishment for mortal sin, is described in such horrid detail that the listeners are driven to confession and contrition. Then follows the consolation: God has forgiven, the beauty of paradise is evoked, and with holy communion the grace of God descends into the souls of the former sinners. Grace will help them to steer clear of mortal sins in the future, and should the devil be victorious again, grace can be won back at once by confession, contrition, and communion. By taking part in the retreat, Stephen is driven to confession and communion. He is an idealist and not prepared to do things by halves: he considers becoming a priest.

Chapter 4 is decisive. Stephen has no vocation to become a priest; his vocation is to become an artist. The shock of recognition hits him when he watches a girl on the beach.

She seemed like one whom magic had changed into the likeness of a strange and beautiful seabird. Her long slender bare legs were delicate as a crane's and pure save where an emerald trail of seaweed had fashioned itself as a sign upon her flesh. Her thighs, fuller and softhued as ivory, were bared almost to the hips where the white fringes of her

drawers were like featherings of soft white down. Her
slateblue skirts were kilted boldly about her waist and dove-
tailed behind her. Her bosom was a bird's soft and slight,
slight and soft as the breast of some darkplumaged dove.
But her long fair hair was girlish: and girlish, and touched
with the wonder of mortal beauty, her face.[10]

He knows now that he will be an artist, that he will
live the sensual life. Of course, this does not seem to
be a reason for anyone to leave the Church. But we
must not forget that Stephen is an idealist. He
knows that he will commit sins (like everybody
else) but he cannot (like everybody else) accept the
hypocrisy of pretending to regret and confess that
which he does not regret and which he knows he
will do again as soon as temptation arises.

Chapter 5 presents Stephen as a young man, a
strong personality, free of superstitions, free of religious prejudices. He meets his clergyman professors
as an equal. Church-ridden Ireland is not the place
for an artist of his kind. He has no sympathies with
art on a nationalistic scale. He prepares to leave for
the Continent. Stephen's hatred of the clergy seems
to be insufficiently motivated. We must keep in
mind that Stephen's hatred is really Joyce's, and
Joyce had a personal reason to distrust any priest.
Nora had told him that a priest in Galway had taken
her on his knees (she was sixteen at the time) and
had put his hand under her skirt. He had then told
her to say at confession that a man had done this,
and not to mention that it had been a priest. As late
as 1909, Joyce was still jealous of this occurrence.
He wrote to her on October 27: "I see nothing on
every side of me but the image of the adulterous

priest and his servants and of sly deceitful women.
. . . Perhaps if you were with me I would not
suffer so much. Yet sometimes when that horrible
story of your girlhood crosses my mind the doubt
assails me that even you are secretly against me." [11]
This, because Nora, reasonable as she was, could not
extend the sin of one priest to all priests. When she
and Joyce passed a priest in Trieste, Joyce asked
her: "Do you not find a kind of repulsion or disgust
at the sight of one of those men?" Nora answered:
"No, I don't." Hence Joyce's suspicion that even
she might be "secretly against me" and eventually
betray him. This motive for Joyce's hatred is transferred to Stephen Dedalus, but it could not be so
motivated since Joyce did not introduce Nora's
counterpart into *A Portrait*.

   In Chapter 5, Stephen subjects himself to a rig-
orous self-analysis. The insights he gains into his
own character may without doubt be taken as valid
for Joyce's character as well. What Cranly (Byrne)
says about Stephen, is also true of Joyce: "It is a
curious thing, do you know . . . how your mind is
super-saturated with the religion in which you say
you disbelieve." [12] Like Stephen, Joyce decided before his departure: "I will not serve that in which I
no longer believe whether it call itself my home,
my fatherland or my church: and I will try to express myself in some mode of life or art as freely as
I can and as wholly as I can, using for my defense
the only arms I allow myself to use—silence, exile,
and cunning." [13]

3

Zurich

When war broke out in 1914, it hardly affected Joyce at first. He continued teaching at the school of commerce, gave private lessons, and worked part-time as English correspondent for a business firm. Stanislaus, who was an outspoken Irredentist, was arrested on January 9, 1915. He was detained in Austria until 1918. Eileen married a Czech bank cashier and went to live in Prague. When Italy entered the war in May 1915, Joyce had completed his play *Exiles* and was working on the third chapter of *Ulysses*. Many of Joyce's pupils returned to their own countries, the school of commerce was closed, and in June the Joyce family went to Switzerland. Influential friends and the American consul in Trieste had helped with visas and permits.

During the next few years, Joyce lived mainly from grants and donations. Nora's uncle Michael Healy helped; Pound, Yeats, and George Gissing procured £75 for Joyce from the Royal Literary Fund. Pound sent him £50 privately and succeeded in persuading the Society of Authors to pay him £52 in weekly installments for six months. Yeats, George Moore, and Edward Marsh procured £100 from the Civil List. John Quinn in New York bought Joyce's manuscripts. Harriet Weaver sent him £200 anonymously and then presented him with a war bond of £5000 which paid Joyce £62 10 s. every three months. Mrs. Edith McCormick gave him 1000 Swiss francs a month for a year and a half. When he pretended to be in legal trouble (the claim was less than $40), American friends sent him

$1000. With all this, Joyce could now live quite comfortably. His aggregate income during his Zurich years was, in fact, about four times as high as the income of the average Swiss family.

With *A Portrait of the Artist as a Young Man*, Joyce had no luck in England. J. B. Pinker, who was also D. H. Lawrence's agent, tried to place the book with several publishers. Edward Garnett—who had recognized the talents of Lawrence and Conrad— read the book for the firm of Duckworth, but his report was anything but enthusiastic. No printer or publisher wanted to touch this potentially dangerous manuscript; after the proceedings against Lawrence's novel *The Rainbow* one could not be careful enough. Luckily, B. W. Huebsch, an enterprising young American publisher, took an interest in Joyce and decided to bring out *Dubliners* and *A Portrait* in 1916. As no English publisher could be found, Harriet Weaver decided to import sheets of the American edition and distribute the book itself.

It is strange to believe that Joyce—who seemed to know everybody in Zurich—had no relations with the Dadaists. He met René Schickele, Ivan Goll, and Frank Wedekind, but he did not mention Hans Arp, Hugo Ball, or Tristan Tzara in his letters, nor did they have any friends in common. This is all the more astonishing since most of the Dadaists and Joyce belonged to refugee circles. What Joyce would later do with words in *Finnegans Wake*, Hans Arp was then doing in Zurich. Arp's Dadaist poetry could, indeed, be interpreted as a preliminary exercise for *Finnegans Wake*. Some critics concluded, to Joyce's amusement, that he must have been among the founding fathers of Dadaism.[1] Joyce had had no contact with the Italian Futurists either. He used the word "futuristic" in 1918 when he asked Frank Budgen whether the Cyclops episode in *Ulysses* was not "futuristic." He evidently had no idea of what Marinetti and his followers were, in fact, preaching. Joyce cared nothing for literary movements, not even Irish ones. He did not care about the war either; in his letters there are almost no references to the military or political news of the day.

Among his Zurich friends, Joyce's favorite one was Frank Budgen, a painter. Budgen has written an account of Joyce's Zurich years in Chapters 1, 2, and 10 of his book, *James Joyce and the Making of Ulysses*. The other chapters are a commentary on *Ulysses*. Budgen was the most initiated person as far as the writing of *Ulysses* is concerned. While Joyce was in Zurich he followed the progress of the novel chapter by chapter. By his patient listening and his stimulating discussion, he became so indispensable to Joyce that he later tried to persuade Budgen to come and join him in Trieste. Joyce even offered to pay half the fare. We know from Budgen that Flaubert rated highest in Joyce's literary canon; he also liked Tolstoy, Jacobsen, and D'Annunzio. On the other hand, he had little regard for Dostoevsky and Balzac.

Before concentrating all his effort on the construction of *Ulysses*, Joyce completed the only one of his dramas which has been preserved, *Exiles*. Like

the dramatic attempts of his great fellow novelists—
D. H. Lawrence, Joseph Conrad, and Henry
James—*Exiles* was a failure. It is interesting to note
that Joyce, who had expressed reservations about
his poetry and *Dubliners*, was always convinced of
the high quality of *Exiles*. What happens in the
play? The action takes place in Dublin in 1912.
Richard Rowan, a writer, returns to Ireland from
exile. He is accompanied by his wife, Bertha, and his
eight-year-old son, Archie. Several years ago he had
left Ireland with Bertha—without having married
her; the child is not baptized. These facts had hastened the death of Rowan's mother, who had been a
devout Catholic. It is obvious that the persons and
the situation are largely autobiographical. His former friend, the journalist Robert Hand, approaches
Rowan again. He had courted Bertha before her
elopement and now brings her roses. While he tries
to seduce her, he also attempts to get a professorship
for Richard at the university. He is at the same time
a friend and a Judas. Hand, of course, is largely a
portrait of Cosgrave, who had falsely asserted that
he had once been in Nora's favor. The situation,
however, is not depicted as it really was, but as it
would have been if Cosgrave's assertion about his
former relationship with Nora had been true.

Bertha is intellectually unassuming but natural
and honest; she tells her husband straightaway
about Robert's intentions. Richard does not seem to
be greatly disturbed; he leaves it to his wife to do
what she thinks best. He pretends that he does not
care whether she is going to deceive him or not;

whatever turn events will take, he will pretend to be amused. As a contrast to Bertha, a female intellectual named Beatrice is introduced: she is intelligent but lifeless; she loves Richard and is intellectually his equal. Bertha, who is disturbed by her husband's wishy-washy attitude, goes to see Robert. Richard, however, spoils Robert's fun by turning up in person before this rendezvous and letting Robert know that he is fully aware of his dishonorable intentions. It therefore seems probable that nothing whatever happened during Bertha's visit to Robert. In the future, however, Richard will be able to enjoy doubting his wife's faithfulness to him. Despite her honesty, it is still possible that she had given herself to Robert on that occasion and had deceived him. Richard thus appears as a masochist and an intellectually very limited man. But it is clear that Joyce had intended him to be a man of above average ability, a "portrait of the artist," as a man in the prime of his life.

In his introduction to the play, Padraic Colum says: "In its structure, *Exiles* is a series of confessions; the dialogue has the dryness of recitals in the confessional; its end is an act of contrition." [2] Joyce had written a series of notes about the play which appears as an appendix in more recent editions of the play. One of these notes reads as follows: "The play, a rough and tumble between the Marquis de Sade and Freiherr v. Sacher-Masoch. Had not Robert better give Bertha a little bite when they kiss? Richard's masochism needs no example." [3] The play is a meditation about human relations. One can get

to the core of Joyce's thinking by analyzing the
events chronologically. Bertha had the choice of
staying in Ireland with Robert Hand or of leaving
with Richard Rowan. She preferred to leave with
Rowan. But Bertha's life with Richard proved to be
none too happy, and Rowan suspected that she
might since have regretted not marrying Robert.
Being a generous person, he gives her a chance to
leave him and attach herself to Robert. It is clear
that, despite her occasional unhappiness, she is still in
love with Rowan. But she is unable to interpret his apparent unconcern about her fidelity as generosity on
his part. She is phlegmatic and not too bright, down
to earth and not able to understand Rowan's thinking. She can explain his attitude in two ways only:
either he is tired of her and wants to be free himself
—to marry Beatrice; or else he has become plain
mad. Robert wishes Rowan well, it seems, but
would like to get his hands on Bertha. Joyce meditated on the following possibilities: Robert is Rowan's disciple who will betray him. Cannot Robert
still be his friend? Should not Rowan be above
the traditional one-man-for-one-woman morality?
Could their friendship not become greater in sharing
the same woman? Would Bertha not enjoy having
an affair with Robert and has he a right to forbid her
this pleasure—especially since he has not married
her? Richard is obsessed by an idea and a passion.
His idea is this: "But that I will reproach myself
then for having taken all for myself because I would
not suffer her to give to another what was hers and
not mine to give, because I accepted from her her

loyalty and made her life poorer in love. That is my
fear. That I stand between her and any moments of
life that should be hers, between her and you, between her and anyone, between her and anything. I
will not do it." [4] And his passion: "That is what I
must tell you too. Because in the very core of my
ignoble heart I longed to be betrayed by you and by
her—in the dark, in the night—secretly, meanly,
craftily. By you, my best friend, and by her." [5]
This last speech could have been made by King
Marke in Georg Kaiser's drama *König Hahnrei*
(1913), another transformation of the theme of
Tristan and Isolde. Marke, too, had longed to be
betrayed by his wife and by his best friend. But
when they got tired of their affair and stopped be-
traying the king, he killed them. Richard Rowan is
much more subtle. He does not want his wife to
betray him and interferes at the critical moment.
But he can now tell himself that she still *may* have
betrayed him. In fact, this masochist has managed to
have his cake and eat it too.

  Robert is, in fact, the one who gets short-changed
by everybody. Whatever he says to Bertha in confi-
dence she reports to her husband at once. She en-
courages his passion for her—but with no intention
of fulfilling it. Robert finally sees through Richard,
and says to Bertha: ". . . he longs to be delivered.
. . . From every law, Bertha, from every bond. All
his life he has sought to deliver himself. Every chain
but one he has broken and that one we are to break,
Bertha—you and I." [6] This may be the final explanation: Rowan wants to be completely independent,

completely invulnerable. His (conventional) love attachment to Bertha makes him vulnerable. If he can bring himself to the point where he can accept with equanimity the thought that she is sleeping with Robert Hand—then he will be completely free: the perfect stoic. Nobody will be able to hurt him any more.

In 1918, in the March issue of the *Little Review*, edited by Margaret Anderson and Jane Heap in New York, the first pages of *Ulysses* appeared— the novel which was to become one of the most widely discussed books of the twentieth century. The publication was due to Ezra Pound's good services. What Harriet Weaver had done for *A Portrait*, the editors of the *Little Review* did for *Ulysses*. They published the novel as a series and did not give up even when, as happened four times, a number of the periodical was confiscated by the censors. However, in September 1920 the New York Society for the Prevention of Vice instigated legal action, and the two editors were fined $50 each and had to abandon their plan to bring out the last chapters of the novel. Although Joyce was now working more intensively on *Ulysses* than ever before, he did not give up all other activities. Together with Claud W. Sykes he founded the "English Players," a troupe of mostly amateur actors who staged several English plays in Swiss cities. He had hoped that they would eventually perform *Exiles*—but they did not. Nevertheless, Joyce spent a great deal of time and money on the venture, which could have been more successful if the English consulate had not boy-

cotted the performances. The reason was that Joyce
had quarreled with one of their employees, Henry
Carr, who wanted the players to pay for his new
suit which he had bought (he said) solely in order
to perform his part. Carr lost this case in court, but
he won another one against Joyce. Joyce had said
that Carr had insulted him verbally, but Joyce could
not produce witnesses and was condemned to pay
179 Swiss francs. He refused to pay and was let off
with 50 francs by the lenient Swiss authorities.

In May 1918, *Exiles* was published by Grant
Richards in London and by B. W. Huebsch in New
York. Stefan Zweig congratulated Joyce on the
play; it was translated into German and staged in
Munich on August 7, 1919. After 1917, Joyce's eyes
rapidly became worse; sometimes he suffered such
pain that reading became impossible and writing
very hard as well. On August 18, 1917, he suffered
an attack of glaucoma and had to be operated on.
(Ten other operations took place between 1923 and
1930.) After the operation, Joyce tried the milder
climate of Locarno for a few months but came back
to Zurich in January 1918; Locarno was too quiet a
place in winter. In late 1918, Joyce fell in love with
Marthe Fleischmann, a Swiss girl who lived near his
own apartment. He wrote her a few letters in
French and German which have been preserved by
Heinrich Straumann, Professor of English Literature at the University of Zurich. She was the mis-
tress of an engineer and had no feelings for Joyce;
the affair remained one-sided and necessarily pla-
tonic. When the engineer finally found out, Joyce

apparently did not have too much trouble soothing his feelings. Nora knew nothing of the affair. She was more interested in her penny novelettes than in *Ulysses*, which was—for her—a heap of rubbish. Budgen wrote that she treated Joyce as if he were a naughty child. She pitied his preoccupation with cloacal matters and was disgusted at his fascination with obscene words.

In October 1919, Joyce went to Trieste with his family. Stanislaus, released in 1918, was there already. So was the family of his sister Eileen who had come back from Prague. Stanislaus had become older and had lost some of his idealism: he refused to be made use of by his brother any longer. Several parts of *Ulysses* he criticized quite harshly, and throughout his life he held *Finnegans Wake* to be a literary fraud. Joyce once more gave English lessons and regained his former position at the school of commerce. But teaching was too much of a burden to him now; he needed all his reserves for *Ulysses*. Ezra Pound, whom he visited at Lake Garda, suggested that he should go to live in Paris. Joyce liked the idea and arrived in Paris on July 8, 1920. The French capital was to be his home for the next twenty years.

4

Constructing
Ulysses

Pound had made considerable propaganda for Joyce, and his name was soon well known in Paris literary circles. Pound got Madame Bloch-Savitsky to translate *A Portrait of the Artist as a Young Man* into French. The novel appeared in 1924 as *Dedalus* (Editions de la Sirène). Joyce was less lucky with the French translation of *Exiles*, made by Jenny Serruys. She got A. F. Lugné-Poë (Théâtre de l'Oeuvre) interested; at first he promised to stage the play but abandoned the idea definitely in June 1921. Madame Bloch-Savitsky lent Joyce her apartment for a few months. He had spent all his money on the trip from Trieste and had to borrow right and left. Pound helped with cash, somebody lent a bed, and Miss Weaver gave Joyce the interest on another £3500. If he had known how to plan ahead, Joyce could have easily lived on the income from Miss Weaver alone. Sylvia Beach and Adrienne Monnier were now added to the list of useful friends; both were booksellers. When all attempts in England and America had failed, Sylvia Beach took it upon herself to publish *Ulysses*. T. S. Eliot and Wyndham Lewis visited Joyce, and their positive opinions about *Ulysses* (Wyndham Lewis later changed his mind) increased Joyce's prestige considerably. Among his friends, Valery Larbaud was the most important one. He wrote—under Joyce's guidance and supervision—the first interpretation of *Ulysses*.

Joyce went through five sets of proofs. He corrected and enlarged feverishly. Richard Ellmann says that "The book grew by one third in proof."[1]

His eyes bothered him again, and he had his usual financial worries, although Miss Weaver sent him £200 as an advance on the English edition; Larbaud lent him his apartment, and the American author Robert McAlmon, a new friend provided him with considerable sums of money. Joyce wanted *Ulysses* to appear on his fortieth birthday, February 2, 1922. On that day the first two copies arrived in Paris from Dijon, where the book was printed. The rest of the edition went on the market a few weeks later.

The publication of the novel had been carefully prepared. The censor's proceedings against the *Little Review* were used as a preliminary advertisement. The original edition consisted of 1000 copies. One hundred copies, signed by Joyce, sold for 350 francs, 150 copies (on special paper) for 250 francs, and the remaining 750 copies for 150 francs. The edition was sold by subscription. Joyce was to receive two thirds of the net profits. On December 7, 1921, Larbaud gave a lecture about Joyce and his forthcoming novel in Miss Beach's bookshop. Two hundred and fifty people attended, and many of them subscribed. Miss Beach's edition was soon sold out. On March 20, 1922, only 130 copies were left. Miss Weaver had decided to distribute a second edition of 2000 copies in England and America under the imprint of the Egoist Press. The books were sent out from Paris. It seems that only about 1500 copies reached their destinations safely. The rest was held up by the U. S. Post Office and burned. Miss Weaver printed another 500 copies, but almost all of these were caught by the English customs at Folkestone.

It may be supposed that many buyers who had been looking forward to new thrills in pornographic reading were disappointed. *Ulysses* is difficult to read and stimulates the sexual appetites of very few people. Although some Joyceans assert the opposite, most critics agree that it is a mistake to read *Ulysses* without preparation. Some kind of a key is essential. What is the novel about, what are the contents, and what is the structure like? The book has eighteen chapters, of which the first three form an introduction and the last three an epilogue. The introduction treats of Stephen (Telemachus); the main part (12 chapters) is dedicated to Bloom's adventures (the travels of Ulysses), and the epilogue describes the homecoming (Ithaca and Penelope). Stanley Sultan argues convincingly (*The Argument of Ulysses*, 1964) that the middle section consists of again three parts: Chapters 4 to 9, Chapter 10 (an intermezzo), and Chapters 10 to 15. At first Joyce had given his chapters headings, but later in the printed version he had left them out. The titles, however, are useful, and in critical works about Joyce these titles are used to refer to a chapter. The action closely parallels Homer's *Odyssey*; seventeen chapters refer to specific episodes in the Greek epic.

Detailed, chapter-by-chapter interpretations of *Ulysses* can be found in Paul Jordan Smith's *A Key to the Ulysses of James Joyce*, in Frank Budgen's *The Making of Ulysses*, in Stuart Gilbert's *James Joyce's Ulysses*, and in Harry Blamires' *The Bloomsday Book: A Guide through Joyce's Ulysses*. Among the best book-long interpretations are *The*

Argument of Ulysses by Stanley Sultan, *Surface and Symbol: The Consistency of James Joyce's Ulysses* by Robert Martin Adams, *Fabulous Voyager: a Study of James Joyce's Ulysses* by Richard M. Kain, and *The Classical Temper: A Study of James Joyce's Ulysses* by S. L. Goldberg. Also very interesting are the chapters on *Ulysses* in Walton Litz's *The Art of James Joyce: Method and Design in Ulysses and Finnegans Wake.* The table on the following page (set up by Joyce himself) about the technique and the symbols used in the novel may be sufficient for a first reading, provided the reader is well acquainted with Homer's *Odyssey.* The titles of the episodes are important because they help in looking up the relevant episode in Homer (or in an encyclopedia of Greek mythology). The entries under the headings of place, time, and art could have been thought out by really attentive readers without Joyce's help. The entries under the headings of organs, colors, and symbols are helpful, but if Joyce himself had not provided them, no one would have guessed their existence. The question arises at once: How useful are symbols in a novel which can have no meaning for anybody except for the author? In what way can they contribute to the value of a work of art? Joyceans will say that, in the case of *Ulysses,* Joyce has provided his readers with everything they need to understand the symbolic content. All they have to do is to read Stuart Gilbert's guide —inspired and approved by Joyce himself.

An interesting and readable chapter about the symbolic meaning of *Ulysses* is contained in Wil-

List of Symbols for Ulysses [2]

Title [2]	Scene	Hour	Organ
1. Telemachus	The Tower	8 A.M.	
2. Nestor	The School	10 A.M.	
3. Proteus	The Strand	11 A.M.	
4. Calypso	The House	8 A.M.	Kidney
5. Lotus-eaters	The Bath	10 A.M.	Genitals
6. Hades	The Graveyard	11 A.M.	Heart
7. Aeolus	The Newspaper	12 noon	Lungs
8. Lestrygonians	The Lunch	1 P.M.	Esophagus
9. Scylla and Charybdis	The Library	2 P.M.	Brain
10. Wandering Rocks	The Streets	3 P.M.	Blood
11. Sirens	The Concert Room	4 P.M.	Ear
12. Cyclops	The Tavern	5 P.M.	Muscle
13. Nausicaa	The Rocks	8 P.M.	Eye, Nose
14. Oxen of the Sun	The Hospital	10 P.M.	Womb
15. Circe	The Brothel	12 midnight	Locomotor Apparatus
16. Eumaeus	The Shelter	1 A.M.	Nerves
17. Ithaca	The House	2 A.M.	Skeleton
18. Penelope	The Bed		Flesh

Art	Color	Symbol	Technique
Theology	White, gold	Heir	Narrative (young)
History	Brown	Horse	Catechism (personal)
Philology	Green	Tide	Monologue (male)
Economics	Orange	Nymph	Narrative (mature)
Botany, Chemistry		Eucharist	Narcissism
Religion	White, black	Caretaker	Incubism
Rhetoric	Red	Editor	Enthymemic
Architecture		Constables	Peristaltic
Literature		Stratford, London	Dialectic
Mechanics		Citizens	Labyrinth
Music		Barmaids	*Fuga per canonem*
Politics		Fenian	Gigantism
Painting	Grey, blue	Virgin	Tumescence, detumescence
Medicine	White	Mothers	Embryonic development
Magic		Whore	Hallucination
Navigation		Sailors	Narrative (old)
Science		Comets	Catechism (impersonal)
		Earth	Monologue (female)

liam York Tindall's *A Reader's Guide to James
Joyce*. Tindall investigates hundreds of possible
symbols. Few Joyceans would feel how preposter-
ous Tindall's following statement really is: "One
reading does not work, we readily agree, for works
of Mann, Proust, Faulkner, or Conrad. [Why not?]
After many readings of *Ulysses*, we should be ready
to agree that many readings are insufficient. Return-
ing to it again and again, we must pause at each sentence, every word, asking why and learning more
and more, but never all. Even this reward, however,
is worth the trouble." [3] To understand every allu-
sion in *Ulysses* (and *Finnegans Wake*) is impossible;
only Joyce himself could do this. But by studying
every detail of his and his friends' biographies, by
reading all the books and newspapers he had read—
in short, by reliving Joyce's life—it is possible to
identify a good deal of the allusions in *Ulysses* and
Finnegans Wake. Is it worth the effort?

   Ninety-nine percent of Joyce's readers are not
Joyceans. They want to read his works once and
then switch to Goethe, Molière, and others. They
may save time and avoid despair by having a careful
look at the list of symbols and by going through a
concise summing-up of each chapter before actually
reading it. Before we turn to a discussion of the
whole work, let us look at the contents of the
eighteen chapters because in the case of *Ulysses* an
understanding of what happens is the first aim of
any interpretation.

CHAPTER 1   *Telemachus*.   We are in the Martello
Tower, a few miles from Dublin, on the seashore. It

is eight o'clock in the morning. The characters who appear are: Stephen Dedalus whom we know from *A Portrait*; somewhat older and back from his exile in Paris (model: Joyce); Buck Mulligan, superior to Stephen in wit but not in artistic talent and intelligence (model: Oliver Gogarty); and Haines, an English friend of Mulligan's. Mulligan reproaches Stephen for having refused to kneel down and pray when his mother died. But he is a blasphemer himself: he handles his shaving pot like a chalice, chanting (in Latin) bits from the beginning of the Mass. Stephen has left the Church and his family, but he is not enthusiastic about Mulligan's sacrilegious chant. A woman brings milk, and Mulligan swims in the sea. Stephen is not satisfied with his friends and wants to leave the tower. There is little action beyond this; much is dialogue. Like everything else in Joyce, this chapter is made up almost exclusively of autobiographical elements, but elements which here are given a symbolical meaning. Parallels with Homer are: Stephen is Telemachus; Buck Mulligan and Haines are Penelope's suitors, Antinous and Elpenor. Other symbols: the old woman is blinded Ireland who nurses (gives milk to) her conqueror (Haines, the Englishman) and her betrayer (Buck Mulligan). Milk (and cows) are leitmotifs throughout the book. Other parallels are: Stephen = Hamlet; the old woman = Athenae; Stephen = Christ; and Mulligan = Judas.

CHAPTER 2 *Nestor*.   Joyce had once taught for a few weeks at the Clifton School in Dalkey. This school is the scene. Stephen is teaching. Later he goes to collect his salary. Headmaster Deasy (Nestor) gives him some practical advice and a letter about foot and mouth disease which Stephen is asked to get published in a newspaper. In the *Odyssey*, Telemachus had visited his father's old friend Nestor in order to ask him where his father might be found. Nestor had sent him to Menelaus. Deasy is quite happy with his superficial life; he is anti-Semitic.

CHAPTER 3 *Proteus*. Stephen goes walking on the beach at Sandymount and soliloquizes. Proteus was an Egyptian god of the sea who had given evasive replies about Odysseus' whereabouts. In Joyce's chapter Stephen is alone. The place of Proteus is taken by Stephen's rapidly moving thoughts. To illustrate Proteus' evasive replies, Joyce uses fragments from several languages (French, German, Latin, Spanish, Italian, etc.). The young man's interior monologue here will be paralleled by similar monologues of Bloom and, finally, by that of the mature woman in the last chapter.

CHAPTER 4 *Calypso*. After the three introductory chapters of the Telemachia, Bloom (Odysseus) is now introduced for the first time. He is a Jew who earns his living as an advertising agent with a newspaper. He is married to Molly, a pretty singer, who for years has been refusing to have sexual intercourse with him; she has an affair with Blazes Boylan, her manager. Bloom feeds the cat, goes to the butcher's, buys a piece of kidney, and fries it. He takes breakfast to Molly in bed and reads a letter from his daughter, Milly. Molly has a letter from her lover Boylan who says that he will come around at four o'clock to rehearse "Love's Old Sweet Song." Bloom leaves the house dressed in black, intending to attend Paddy Dignam's funeral. Calypso casts a spell on Ulysses and keeps him with her for several years. As Ulysses longs for Penelope, so Bloom longs for sexual union with his wife. Much in *Ulysses* is parody; it is ironical that it is not Calypso but Penelope herself who keeps Ulysses at a distance. Molly is Calypso (She still fascinates Bloom and treats him like a slave) *and* Penelope (his lawful wife).

CHAPTER 5 *The Lotus Eaters.* In Homer, Odysseus and his companions go on land and eat lotus plants. The effect of this plant is to make those who eat of it forget their homeland. Odysseus drives his companions back on board by force. In Joyce's version, Bloom goes to the post office to collect a letter from Martha Clifford, a woman with whom he would like to have an affair and with whom he carries on a secret correspondence. He buys himself a bar of soap at the druggist's and then goes to the public baths. The parallel with Homer is to be found in the alluring drugs in the chemist's. Some of the symbols in this chapter may be offensive to Christian readers: Bloom's body in the bathtub is compared to the host in the chalice. "This is my body," thinks Bloom, looking at "his navel, bud of flesh." [4]

62   *James Joyce*

CHAPTER 6 *Hades.* The realm of the dead is the cemetery of Glasnevin where Paddy Dignam is being buried. The cab, in which Stephen's father, Simon Dedalus, and two other acquaintances join Bloom, rolls through the city of Dublin. Stephen meets it on his way, so does Blazes Boylan. The conversation in the cab between the four Irishmen is one of the most amusing parts of the book.

CHAPTER 7 *Aeolus.* The friendly god handed Odysseus the unfavorable winds in a bag so that they could not disturb his return journey. Before arriving in Ithaca, however, Odysseus fell asleep, and his companions unwittingly opened the bag of winds. In no time at all the storms drove the ship back to the island of Aeolus, who this time received Odysseus in a rage. In Joyce, Aeolus is the editor-in-chief, Myles Crawford, who at noon is very kind to Bloom. While Bloom is away, Stephen comes with Deasy's letter about the foot and mouth disease. Stephen invites the whole company for a beer. Just as they are on their way, Bloom returns; Crawford, who does not want to be disturbed, dismisses him coarsely. Joyce has worked into this chapter a history of headline techniques used since the eighteenth century. The chapter is filled with the noise of the streets, the trams, the printing presses. The newspaper building represents the lungs of Dublin. News comes in, is printed, and distributed by shouting newsboys.

CHAPTER 8 *The Lestrygonians.* These were gigantic, unappetizing man-eaters who devoured some of Odysseus' companions. The parallel here is provided by the greedy guests in Burton's guest-house. Bloom does not sit down with them but prefers to go on to Davy Byrne's pub to eat a sandwich. He helps a blind young man across the street and decides to visit the museum to have a look at the statues of some nude goddesses. He tries to avoid Blazes Boylan who is on his way to the real Venus, Molly Bloom. In this chapter Joyce made use of a large culinary vocabulary.

CHAPTER 9 *Scylla and Charybdis.* Odysseus' ship had to pass between Charybdis, the pernicious whirlpool, and Scylla, the six-headed monster who sits on a rock. Similarly Bloom, who has visited the Irish National Library, must pass between Stephen and Mulligan who are standing at the entrance. Stephen is the monster sitting on his Aristotelian rock, and Mulligan might be Charybdis. Stephen's theories on Shakespeare have already been mentioned in *A Portrait*. Most of the chapter is taken up by a discussion of Shakespeare. Was Shakespeare Hamlet, Hamlet's father, or both? Was he cuckolded by his brothers? The parallels: God is at the same time God the Father and the Son. Similarly, Joyce is projected into Stephen Dedalus *and* Leopold Bloom, Stephen's spiritual father.

CHAPTER 10 *The Wandering Rocks.* These do not actually appear in the *Odyssey*, but Jason's ship, the *Argo*, passes by them. Circe had warned Odysseus, and he avoids them by going through Scylla and Charybdis. This is the central chapter of *Ulys-*

ses; it has nineteen parts (Stuart Gilbert says eighteen parts and a coda), all of which describe people
and scenes in Dublin. Most of the characters are
known to us from elsewhere. The "Wandering
Rocks" are represented by Dubliners on the move.
The first described is Father Conmee, Rector of
Clongowes Wood. Molly Bloom appears in Section
3, giving a coin to a begging sailor. In Section 5,
Blazes Boylan buys fruit for Molly; in Section 6 Stephen meets his Italian teacher. In Section 7 we learn
that the date is June 16, 1904. Bloom buys a cheap
and mildly pornographic novel for Molly entitled
Sweets of Sin (Section 10). In Section 13, we meet
Stephen talking to his sister Dilly by a bookcart. She
tells him of the poor and miserable life at home. In
the last section, the viceroy's train passes almost
everybody mentioned in this chapter. Tindall says
that Joyce is probably leading the reader around by
the nose—in a labyrinth without a minotaur. Gilbert
insists that the eighteen parts parallel the eighteen
chapters of the entire book and that the chapter as a
whole is a *Ulysses* in miniature. We know from
Frank Budgen that Joyce wrote the chapter with a
map of Dublin in front of him. On this he had
traced the routes of the viceroy and Father Conmee
in red ink. "He calculated to a minute the time necessary for his characters to cover a given distance of
the city." [5] Within the overall structure of the
novel the chapter clearly serves as an intermezzo.

CHAPTER 11   *The Sirens.*   The main scene is the
Ormond Hotel. It is four o'clock. Simon Dedalus is

playing the piano; Blazes Boylan meets Lenehan, whereupon he starts out to see Molly. The blind man whom we met earlier returns for the tuning fork he had forgotten. Bloom answers Martha's letter and thinks about Blazes and Molly. The seductive Siren, Miss Douce, is the prettier of two barmaids. Ironically, there is no need for filling anybody's ears with wax, nor does Bloom have to be restrained from running into anybody's arms. Miss Douce has no intention of seducing him, quite the opposite. She is horrified at the idea of having to marry a "greasy" Jew. It is her colleague, Miss Kennedy, who plugs her ears (with her fingers).

In writing the chapter, Joyce chose structure and texture from the field of music—a Bach fugue to be exact. This structure is "doubly suitable," says Tindall: "Dublin is on a *Bach* [little river in German] and the word fugue means 'flight' "[Sic!].[6] The episode begins with an overture of two pages which contains most of the themes (fifty-seven according to Harry Blamires) which will occur in the episode. The chapter opens with these lines:

Bronze by gold heard the hoofirons, steelyrining [ringing?]
Imperthnthn thnthnthn.
Chips, picking chips off rocky thumbnail, chips.
Horrid! And gold flushed more.
A husky fivenote blue.
Blew. Blue bloom is on the
Gold pinnacled hair.[7]

It is easy to recognize the sound of several musical instruments on the one hand, and—after one has read the episode—the words serving as leitmotifs in this passage. ("Bronze by gold" are the two heads of Miss Douce and Miss Kennedy who hear the "hoofs" of the viceroy's horses.) The film version of 1967 adds one excellent detail: The clock which, in *Ulysses,* "whirred" and "clacked" is a cuckoo clock, and Bloom watches the bird coming out and shouting at him "cuckold, cuckold!" (There is a cuckoo clock at the end of the Nausicaa episode where it does not fit in half as well.)

CHAPTER 12   *The Cyclops.*   In Homer, the one-eyed giant, Polyphemus, keeps Ulysses and his companions prisoners in his cave. During the night Odysseus deprives the monster of his eye with a burning pole. The Greeks flee the following morning by clinging to the bellies of the sheep. Odysseus mocks the giant from his ship, and the latter hurls a rock at them but misses. In *Ulysses,* this scene takes place in Barney Kiernan's bar. The Citizen is the evil Cyclops. He has a vicious dog with him and is a Fenian and full of hatred against everything English (and Jewish). Some believe—quite erroneously—that Bloom had backed a winner in horseracing, and they expect him to buy drinks for everybody. The burning pole is Bloom's cigar; instead of a rock the Citizen throws a biscuit tin after Bloom but, like Polyphemus, does not hit him. Bloom escapes on an open car, the dog chasing after him. The chapter is written in a style of exaggerated pathos, which is hilarious to read.

CHAPTER 13   *Nausicaa.*   In Homer's epos, Nausicaa is the daughter of King Alcinous of the Phaeacians, who kindly looks after Odysseus after he has been washed ashore. Bloom is sitting on the beach at Sandymount. He watches the eighteen-year-old Gerty MacDowell, who is sitting with other children on a cliff, dangling her legs in an exhibitionist way. She excites him to the point of masturbation. In the first part Bloom is seen through her eyes, and the style is that of a cheap novel—well adapted to Gerty's level of intelligence. The second part consists of Bloom's interior monologue. He is quite shocked when he recognizes later on that Gerty has a stiff leg.

CHAPTER 14   *Oxen of the Sun.*   Bloom pays a visit to the maternity hospital and there meets Stephen, Mulligan, and other students who are telling each other dirty jokes and talking about birth control. They offend the god of fertility just as Odysseus' companions had offended Helios by eating his oxen. Bloom waits until Mrs. Purefoy, whose labor has been going on for three days, gives birth to her child. He takes it upon himself to keep a protective eye on the son of his friend, Simon Dedalus, since Stephen appears to be drunk. He accompanies the young people to Burke's pub and afterward follows Stephen and Lynch into the brothel district. This episode contains the complete vocabulary needed for a detailed description of a stock of cattle. It is divided into nine parts that correspond to the nine months of embryonic development. Having a medical dictionary at hand is helpful when reading this chapter. In addition, Joyce also imitates English Literary language from Old English to the end of the nineteenth century, another parallel of embryonic growth. John Greenway gives the following list of works and authors Joyce parodies in the sixty pages of this chapter: Anglo-Saxon and Middle English writings, Mandeville, Malory, Sir Thomas More, *Euphues*, Spenser, the Bible (King James Version), Browne's liturgy, Bunyan, Pepys, Swift, Sterne, Addison, Goldsmith, Burke, Gibbon, medical jargon of the nineteenth century, the Gothic novel, Lamb, De Quincey, Coleridge, Landor, Macaulay, scientific jargon, Dickens, Newman, Pater, Ruskin, Carlyle, different kinds of slang, and American evangelistic oratory.[8]

CHAPTER 15   *Circe.*   In Homer, Circe is a sorceress who turns Odysseus' companions into swine. In Joyce, she is Bella Cohen, owner of a brothel. Odysseus was fortified against enchantment by having a magic root with him; Bloom's magic root is a shriveled potato in his pocket. Bloom follows Stephen and Lynch, both drunk, into Bella's salon. Bloom and Stephen have visions, the sources of which, according to Tindall, are to be found partly in Sacher-Masoch's *Venus im Pelz* and in Krafft-Ebing's *Psychopathia Sexualis*. Stephen breaks the lamp with a stick. Bloom, now in his role as an anxious father, makes sure that Stephen is not overcharged by Mrs. Cohen and carries hat and stick after him. Stephen is knocked down by a drunken soldier and abandoned by Lynch (Judas). Bloom is thinking of his own son who had died long ago and takes care of Stephen. This chapter is the most difficult one to read. Al-

though the skeleton of the action is easy to understand, it is filled in with all kinds of transformations,
hallucinations, visions, dreams, memories—a spiritual
witches' Sabbath. When Bloom meets two police-
men, his guilty conscience reacts, and he has a long
vision of how he is accused in court by several
women. He defends himself but is condemned to
hang. In another scene, Bloom sees himself as a great
orator and leader of the Irish people. However, the
people turn against him in the end. Stephen has a
hallucination in which he is the Catholic Primate of
Ireland. Then Bloom has a masochistic vision: he is a
woman, and Bella Cohen changes into a man and
beats and tortures him. The Circe episode takes up
more than a fifth of the book.

CHAPTER 16 *Eumaeus.* When Ulysses arrived in
Ithaca, he first went to the hut of the faithful swineherd Eumaeus. Telemachus met him there; father
and son recognized each other and then went to the
palace to get rid of the suitors. Bloom drags Stephen, who is completely drunk, into a cabman's
shelter where he slowly comes to. The proprietor is
Skin-the-Goat Fitzharris (the swineherd). Stephen
recognizes his spiritual father in Bloom. They discuss all kinds of things and then proceed to Bloom's
house (the castle of Odysseus).

CHAPTER 17 *Ithaca.* This would be the chapter
in which Odysseus took his revenge on the suitors,
and one expects that Bloom should somehow take
his revenge on Boylan (or Stephen on Mulligan).

But there is no violence. Bloom takes Stephen home
with him where he makes cocoa. Stephen turns
down an invitation to sleep there and leaves the
house. Bloom goes to bed, speaks with Molly, and
meditates. He compares himself to a traveler, tells
Molly about his adventures, and falls asleep. The
style is the question-and-answer technique of the
catechism. The answers are ridiculously precise and
often amusingly irrelevant. This was Joyce's favorite episode.

CHAPTER 18 *Penelope*. Molly is dozing, and
Joyce allows the flow of her thoughts to glide past
us without any punctuation—about 25,000 words.
She is supposed to represent Venus, Mary, Penelope, Mother Earth—in short, the "Ewig-Weibliche."
"Yes" is a word she uses often, and it is the last
word of the novel. Molly's thoughts touch on many
things but concentrate on the sexual experiences she
has had with men.

Ulysses is the result of seven years' hard work—
not so much of writing, but of meditating, thinking,
constructing. On the average, Joyce wrote about
half a page (of the final version) per day. The time-
consuming things were collecting information, organizing the material, thinking out the symbolisms
and parallelisms, and revising what had already been
written in the light of new themes or techniques
introduced in later episodes. *Ulysses* is a repository
of all the things Joyce knew—what he had learned in
school, what he had read, what he had been told by

others, what he himself had experienced. It had not been his aim at the beginning to put *everything* into the novel. But once the structure was there and the first episodes were written, the novel could absorb as much as Joyce wanted to put in. "Bloomsday" stood for every day, Bloom for everybody; the novel was truly universal, and so there was nothing in the world which could not be fitted in. It is therefore not surprising that the later episodes are much longer than the earlier ones. In fact, the last five chapters take up as much space as the first thirteen episodes combined. Stanislaus noticed this and wrote to Joyce on August 7, 1924: ". . . as the episodes grow longer and longer and you try to tell every damn thing you know about anybody that appears or anything that crops up my patience oozes out." [9] Stanislaus' reaction is understandable, but the skeleton of the novel is constructed in such a way that the *Encyclopaedia Britannica* (in fact, every known phenomenon in the universe) could be incorporated into it. The miracle is that Joyce could bring in so many trivialities and still succeed in producing an interesting, amusing, and readable piece of literature.

As a result of his years among the Jesuits, Joyce's philosophical and theological knowledge was considerable. He knew his Aristotle, Aquinas, Fathers of the Church, Nietzsche, and Vico. (The last's influence on *Finnegans Wake* is even more important than on *Ulysses* and will be mentioned later.) Joyce's interpretation of the *Odyssey* (especially the Jewish elements) is to some extent based

on Victor Bérard's *Les Phéniciens de l'Odyssée*
(Paris, 1902–3, 2 vols.). Frazer's *Golden Bough* and
Madame Blavatsky were as important to Joyce as to
D. H. Lawrence. The history of Ireland and of the
city of Dublin serves throughout the novel as filling
material. The main reference for the symbolism is
Homer's *Odyssey* itself. Why did Joyce choose it?
If an author wants to create symbolic meanings and
show parallelisms, there is no use in taking an un-
known work (or an obscure historical occurrence)
as a point of departure. The reader would have no
associations in his mind, and the entire symbolism
and parallelism would be lost. There are few works
of literature (or events in history) which are
known to a large portion of Western humanity—for
whom Joyce was writing. The greatest source of
symbolism is the Bible, especially the life of Christ.
Joyce used this source in all his prose works. All
Catholics can be expected to know their missal,
which contains the liturgy of the mass. Joyce knew
it by heart, and in *Ulysses* parodies it again and
again. Non-Catholics will miss something here.
They will not be able to feel the shock a Catholic
feels because for Catholics Joyce's text will often be
blasphemous. In the last lines of "The Lotus Eaters," Bloom pictures himself in the bathtub looking
at his navel and says, "This is my body." These are
the words of Christ on the occasion of the Last Sup-
per, as recorded by St. Matthew 26: 26. They are
spoken at the vital point of every mass, when the
priest lifts the chalice and transforms bread into the
body and wine into the blood of Christ. There is no

doubt that Joyce parodies this scene: the bathtub is the chalice, and Bloom is the host in it. Furthermore, we know from Gilbert (and Joyce) that the main symbol in this episode is the Eucharist. But when I translated these words in line with the German Catholic missal ("Das ist mein Fleisch"), I was attacked at once by an ardent Joycean, Fritz Senn, who said the sentence should be translated as "Dies ist mein Körper" or "Dies ist mein Leib." [10] The first of these sentences also appears in Georg Goyert's German translation of *Ulysses*. "Das ist mein Leib" is at least familiar to those who know Luther's Bible translation, but "Dies ist mein Körper" produces no associations for anyone. This blatant misunderstanding by two eminent Joyceans proves how difficult it is to read Joyce correctly if one does not have the same background—in this case, the same religious background.

But, as mentioned above, the main work of reference—structurally and symbolically—is Homer's *Odyssey*, which Joyce could expect was known to at least the sophisticated reading public. At that time a knowledge of Greek, Latin, and the classical texts was compulsory at most European high schools. In *The Art of James Joyce* (London, 1961), Walton Litz gives an account of Joyce's method of construction in *Ulysses* and in *Finnegans Wake*. Joyce worked with little scraps of paper on which he wrote down ideas as they occurred to him, and he also made notes of quotations and fragments of conversations. When he wrote an episode he took the appropriate bits of paper, ordered them, and copied from them what he wanted to use. When he was done with a particular piece of paper, he would cross out the sentences he had used and would put the paper elsewhere to be used again. In the first version of *Ulysses,* which appeared in the *Egoist* and in the *Little Review* (1918–1920), Joyce had not yet used a fixed list of organs, symbols, colors, and art. This further possibility of symbolism occurred to him later. But once he had adopted it, he inserted this new symbolism into the already finished parts of the book. Several techniques of writing were added later too. The Aeolus chapter, until 1918, consisted of straightforward conventional narrative. Later Joyce made the language fit in with the milieu: he added newspaper headlines, journalistic jargon, symbolism in connection with lungs, and words which convey the sound of wind.

There are only a few other books of world literature that Joyce could have used, such as: the *Aeneid,* the *Divine Comedy, Don Quixote, Faust,* or *Macbeth.* He did use Dante, *Hamlet,* and the life of Shakespeare. By bringing such eminent works of religion and art into relation with trivial occurrences among trivial people on a trivial day, Joyce achieved two things. On the one hand, he parodied the Bible and the *Odyssey* and provoked his readers to either shock or laughter. On the other hand, he lifted trivial happenings and people out of their triviality. June 16, 1904 is not a trivial day any more, and Bloom is a true twentieth-century Odysseus. Joyce took the *Odyssey* down from a high pedestal and immersed it in the present stream of life. It thereby lost some of its strange and distant beauty; to those who had known it well on its pedestal, it may now look ridiculous. On the other hand, it is now nearer to present-day life, available (with proper annotations!) to everybody: one can go and touch it. It looks familiar to us, and it is no less a work of art than Homer's epic. Of course, Joyce was not the only one who chose to construct a modern piece of art by following the pattern of an existing one. Thomas Mann—to mention an author who constructed his works in much the same way as Joyce—used the theme of *Faust* for one of his most important novels. But in spite of all structures and symbolisms—what really makes *Ulysses* fascinating is the language, Joyce's gift for words and rhythm and especially for vivid dialogue. There is not a single verbal cliché in *Ulysses*, except where it is there with the author's blessing (the first part of "Nausicaa").

Many voices have been raised against Joyce's later works. Dr. Carl G. Jung found that *Ulysses* was the work of a man who, like his daughter, tended toward schizophrenia. By writing as he did, he diverted the illness. Wyndham Lewis did not see how anyone could try to record unconscious impressions in the form of words. Let us examine some of the reasons for Joyce's later style. As his letters reveal, Joyce was a rather superficial man, an egoist *in extremis*. In all practical matters he showed little intelligence. His critical writings could have been written by almost any journalist. His knowledge never surpassed the *niveau* of a student holding a bachelor of arts degree from a Jesuit college. No doubt, he was born a literary genius, but having written *Dubliners* and *A Portrait*, he had made use and disposed of the most coherent experiences of his life in Dublin. He felt that if he continued to write, he would have to write about Dublin again. But all there was left in the stores of his memory was a mass of details which could not be formed into a novel along conventional lines—hence the structure of *Ulysses*, the only kind of frame which could give form to the scraps and pieces of information and experiences that Joyce had left and which he could expand by reading old newspapers and the Dublin directory. Still, it needed genius to invent such a structure; and it needed genius to arrange these bits and pieces so that they would become meaningful within the whole and to formulate them so that they would not bore the reader.

The weak point of *Ulysses*, however, is here: Even if the reader has read his Homer, even if he is a Catholic and knows his Bible by heart, he still will not understand every reference in *Ulysses* because he has not lived Joyce's life. As Stanislaus said, Joyce tried, in the end, "to tell every damn thing" he knew.[11] When reading the proofs, he added and added—with the result that Joyce was the first and last person who understood every reference in *Ulysses* (and *Finnegans Wake*). *Ulysses* is not a work for the "new" critics—those who want to ignore the biography of the author. To get close to a complete understanding, one has to know Joyce's biography as exactly as possible; one has to read every book he read, study the life of every person he met, and so on. Is it worth it? No. But even though every passage cannot be understood, *Ulysses* is still worth reading. Joyceans might say that, after all, we do not completely understand our contemporaries either.

One aspect of the novel has never been analyzed in detail: Joyce felt compelled to avenge himself, and his only weapon was his pen. The German author Arno Schmidt has interpreted *Finnegans Wake* as an attack by Joyce on his brother Stanislaus. It certainly is—in part. In *Dubliners* Joyce took vengeance on his native town, in *A Portrait* on the Church, and in *Exiles* on Cosgrave. In *Ulysses* he made sport of everybody against whom he held a grudge—and some others as well. We know that Oliver St. John Gogarty tried to do everything in his power to win back Joyce's friendship for the sole purpose of not being given a negative role in Joyce's forthcoming works. We also know that Joyce rejected any offer of peace—probably because he was jolly well going to use Gogarty (Mulligan) whether he liked it or not. We know from Ellmann's biography that Joyce struck out against people with whom he had quarreled by using their names in unfavorable connections in *Ulysses*. The last chapter can be interpreted as Joyce's retaliation against Nora and women in general because, after all, it mainly reveals the dirtiness of their minds! Indeed, *Ulysses* can be interpreted as Joyce's revenge on Ireland, the Church, and everybody and everything that had contributed to making his life such as it was. *Finnegans Wake* could then be interpreted as the ultimate expression of Joyce's innermost resentments—against the language he had to use, the civilization in which he had to live, and the universe in general.

The publication of *Ulysses* was celebrated by Joyce and his friends in Paris at a dinner; he surprised some of those present by showing them their names in the book. Nora refused to read it. When Joyce gave her a signed copy, she asked to be allowed to sell it straightaway. Joyce read every review of the novel carefully. Whether it was favorable was less important than the fact that he was being discussed. He usually sent a letter of thanks to those whose reviews were favorable. He was more satisfied with T. S. Eliot than with Ezra Pound. The latter found the Homeric parallels unimportant whereas Eliot considered them to have the "importance of a scientific discovery." [12] In England and France, Joyce was generally not taken very seriously at first; by some, the book was considered to be a piece of obscene charlatanry (so for instance by Edward Gosse); Virginia Woolf and George Moore also turned up their noses. The Catholic convert Paul Claudel returned a signed copy without comment. In Dublin, the reaction seems to have been much the same as in Asheville after the publication of Thomas Wolfe's *Look Homeward, Angel. Ulysses* was read in secret so that everybody could find out who was mentioned in it. Yeats, for one, praised it, although he did not finish reading it. Stanislaus read the novel with interest but rejected the Circe chapter:

the most horrible thing in literature, unless you have something on your chest still worse than this "Agony in the Kips." [He goes on:] Isn't your art in danger of becoming a sanitary science. I wish you would write verse again. ...I should think you would need something to restore your self-respect after this last inspection of the stinkpots. Everything dirty seems to have the same irresistible attraction for you that cow-dung has for flies.[13]

Joyce once more showed himself to be a skillful advertiser: He sent copies to friends, asked for their opinion, suggested they write a review, and even provided them with the parts of the text they were to use. *Ulysses* sold well and provided Joyce with a handsome income for the years to come.

Spoonerisms:
Finnegans Wake

Since the Joyces were now quite affluent, Nora suggested they visit Ireland once more. But civil war was going to break out at any moment, and Joyce preferred to stay in Paris. Nora was homesick; after a quarrel with her husband, she left for Ireland on April 1, 1922. Following a ten-day stay in London, she went on to Dublin and from there to Galway. Unfortunately it was just here that the fighting broke out. Nora's bedroom was invaded by soldiers who thought that its window was in a good strategical position. Lying on the floor of a railway carriage, Nora and the children escaped from Galway. In August the family went to London where Joyce met Miss Weaver, his greatest benefactress, for the first time. But after a month the rapidly worsening state of his eyes forced him to return to Paris, where he had his doctor at hand. He was pleased that the second edition of *Ulysses* (2000 copies at £2.2.0 each) was sold out in four days.

In April 1923, Joyce had his teeth extracted, and shortly afterwards he underwent a three-stage operation (sphincterectomy). Even if he could not see much better than before, at least he was not suffering any more pain, and on June 10 the family once more went on a holiday to England. The plans for *Finnegans Wake* were beginning to take shape. On March 10, 1923, he had completed the first two pages of the work that was not to be finished until sixteen years later. Tim Finnegan, who gave the book its title, is the hero of a ballad; he is a hod-carrier and likes alcohol. One morning, while drunk, he falls from a ladder; it looks as if he has broken his neck. His friends lay him out with a gallon of whisky at his feet and a barrel of porter at his head. Then the wake begins and gradually degenerates into a drinking session. The women begin to fight, and someone throws whisky over Finnegan's body; when the hod-carrier smells the familiar drink, he comes back to life.

Joyce was a loving but rather irresponsible father to his children. Lucia was moved from one school to another; she never had a proper home. Giorgio was apprenticed in a bank but was not satisfied with this kind of work. He had a promising bass voice and liked singing so much that he finally decided to enter the Schola Cantorum, where he studied for several years. Occasionally Joyce would devote all his energy supporting artists who he felt deserved more attention than they were getting at the moment. He had saved Edouard Dujardin from oblivion by drawing attention to his novel, *Les Lauriers sont coupés*. He now decided to help his former pupil from Trieste, Ettore Schmitz (Italo Svevo), who in early 1924 had published another excellent but unsuccessful novel: *La Coscienza di Zeno*. Joyce got Valery Larbaud, Benjamin Crémieux, and others to read the novel and write about Svevo. In 1924, the French translation of *A Portrait of the Artist as a Young Man* appeared, and the translation of *Ulysses* was making progress. Most of the work was done by Auguste Morel, and Joyce supervised the progress with a critical eye. Later, he also took an active part in Georg Goyert's German translation. Ford Madox Ford had become editor of the *transatlantic review*, which was published in Paris; it was in this periodical that the first fragment of *Finnegans Wake* appeared (April 1924) under the title given it by Ford, "Work in Progress." In 1925, four other sections of "Work in Progress" appeared in *Contact Collection of Contemporary Writers*, *Criterion*, *This Quarter*, and *Navire d'Argent*.

Once more it was necessary for Joyce to have an operation on his eyes, the most serious up to that time. He recuperated in St. Malo. In November 1924 and in February and April 1925 more operations followed, each more painful than the last; the fact that *Exiles* was finally produced in New York's Neighborhood Playhouse (forty-one performances) was some consolation. The first performances in London took place on February 14 and 15 at the Regent Theatre. G. B. Shaw attended on the second day. In December 1925, Joyce was operated on twice, but the condition of his eyes did not improve. He was now almost completely blind and could only read with the help of strong magnifying glasses. It was impossible for him to dictate *Finnegans Wake*; he had to *see* the words so that he could change their spelling. (In *Finnegans Wake* some words are written back to front, for example, "rabworc" for "crowbar.") Despite all these setbacks he continued working on his book; he revised, made changes, obscured meanings, twisted words, and wrote new parts. The whole thing began to take shape—at least for Joyce.

At Easter 1926, Stanislaus came for a visit. He had written to Joyce in a letter (August 7, 1924) what he thought of *Ulysses* and "Work in Progress." He had praised some parts of *Ulysses* but thought that "Work in Progress" was either the work of a psychopath or a huge literary fraud: "Or perhaps—a sadder supposition—it is the beginning of softening of the brain." [1] Stanislaus was disgusted by the lavish praises of Joyce's devoted circle of admirers. Herbert Gorman held "Work in Progress" to be the last word in modern literature. Stanislaus' comment on that was

It may be the last in another sense, the witless wandering of literature before its final extinction. Not that I imagine that literature will ever die as long as men speak and write. But they may cease to read or at least to read such things. I for one would not read more than a paragraph of it, if I did not know you. [And he added] Why are you still intelligible and sincere in verse? If literature is to develop along the lines of your latest work it will certainly become, as Shakespeare hinted centuries ago, much ado about nothing.[2]

Joyce attempted to change Miss Weaver's critical attitude towards his new work by asking her for instructions on a piece which he could write and build into the book. Thereupon she sent him photos of the Giant's Grave at St. Andrews, Penrith, and asked him to "kindly supply the undersigned with one full length grave account of his esteemed Highness Rhaggrick O'Hoggnor's Hogg Tomb . . ."— nicely parodying Joyce's new style.[3] Joyce went to work and used the product as the opening paragraph of *Finnegans Wake*. The following is an excerpt from the version which Joyce sent to Miss Weaver:

brings us back to Howth Castle & Environs. Sir Tristram,
violer d'amores, had passencore rearrived on the scraggy
isthmus from North Armorica to wielderfight his penisolate war; nor had stream rocks by the Oconee exaggerated themselse to Laurens County, Ga, doublin all the
time; nor avoice from afire bellowsed mishe to tauftauf
thuartpeatrick; . . .[4]

This passage is hardly more comprehensible to
an Englishman than to a German or a Frenchman.
Joyce provided Miss Weaver with a key for it in the
form of a glossary, in which he explains word con-
structions and twisted word formations. The following are a few explanations taken from Joyce's glossary:

passencore=pas encore and *ricorsi storici* of Vico

North Armorica=Brittany

wielderfight=wielderfecten=refight

Dublin, Laurens Co, Georgia, founded by a Dubliner, Peter
Sawyer, on the river Oconee. Its motto: Doubling all the
time

mishe=I am (Irish) i.e. Christian

tauf=to baptize (German)

thuartpeatrick=Thou art Peter and upon this rock etc.[5]

One can, of course, add many other explanations:
"Penisolate," for instance, contains Tristram's
"penis," "Isolde," a "pen," a "peninsular war," etc.

This glossary reveals Joyce's method in writing
Finnegans Wake. Miss Weaver had a point when
she told Joyce in a letter: "But, dear sir, (I always
seem to have a 'but') the worst of it is that without
comprehensive key and glossary, such as you very
kindly made out for me, the poor hapless reader

loses a very great deal of your intention." [6] A few days earlier, Ezra Pound had written that he had made an effort, but: "Nothing so far as I make out, nothing short of divine vision or a new cure for the clapp can possibly be worth all that circumambient peripherization." [7] He was giving up reading "Work in Progress" for the moment but mentioned that he might give it another try at a later date. Joyce tried to justify himself by saying that in the nebulous state of sleep, people could not be depicted in grammatically correct language. By working on it for years, Joyce succeeded in obscuring the passage even further. Here follows the version of the passage as it appears in the final edition of *Finnegans Wake*:

riverrun, past Eve and Adam's, from swerve of shore to bend of bay, brings us by a commodius vicus of recirculation back to Howth Castle and Environs.
Sir Tristram, violer d'amores, fr'over the short sea, had passencore rearrived from North Armorica on this side the scraggy isthmus of Europe Minor to wielderfight his penisolate war: nor had topsawyer's rocks by the stream Oconee exaggerated themselse to Laurens County's gorgios while they went doublin their mumper all the time: nor avoice from afire bellowsed mishe mishe to tauftauf thuartpeatrick: ...[8]

A detailed analysis of this final version can be found in Joseph Campbell and Henry Morton Robinson's *Skeleton Key to Finnegans Wake* (pp. 24–29).

In the years 1926–1928, Joyce had to contend with Samuel Roth, who was publishing parts of *Ulysses* in his periodical *Two Worlds Monthly* without Joyce's permission. Joyce had no copyright in America, since the novel had not yet appeared there and the United States had not signed the Bern agreement on international copyright. He did, however, have some possibilities for action. He collected the signatures of 167 famous authors for a public letter of protest, and he complained that his name had been misused for business purposes without his permission. From then on, Joyce had a few copies of the finished parts of "Work in Progress" printed in America as well, in order to make certain of the copyright. On December 27, 1928, Roth was told by the court that he was not to use Joyce's name in the future. The affair ended in a dispute between Joyce and his lawyers, for he refused to pay more than a third of the fee.

From 1927 on, "Work in Progress" was published as a serial in the Paris periodical *transition*, which had been founded by Eugene Jolas. The parts which had already appeared were printed again—after a thorough revision by Joyce. Because he worked slowly, there often were long intervals between appearances of episodes. Some parts were published as deluxe editions, for instance, *Anna Livia Plurabelle;* Joyce had worked 350 names of rivers into these 20 pages, which, he said to Sisley Huddleston, had taken him 1200 hours to write. Miss Weaver still could not bring herself to like the latest work of her protégé, and Nora, instead of consoling her husband, asked him why he could not write books which people could understand. Also in 1927, Wyndham Lewis attacked Joyce in *Time and Western Man*, and *Pomes Penyeach*, a small group of poems published at twelve francs by Shakespeare & Company, obtained little appreciation from the critics. Joyce rushed to his faithful admirers to have them confirm that he was on the right track, but his belief in *Finnegans Wake* was deeply shaken. He was playing with the idea of abandoning the novel or of letting someone else finish it. This "someone else" was to be James Stephens, an Irishman, whose novels Joyce had read. Stephens and Joyce had some things in common: Christian names, nationality, and birthdays. Stephens was to finish the book in case something happened to Joyce; to this purpose he was initiated into the framework and technique of "Work in Progress."

The German translation of *Ulysses* appeared in 1927. Joyce was not satisfied with it; he had revised parts of the text with Georg Goyert during a stay at Ostend in August 1926. Now, in April 1928, Goyert came to Paris, and Joyce corrected some of the German translation again. The French edition appeared in 1929, published by Adrienne Monnier. After a journey through Austria and Germany on which he met Stanislaus, Joyce's eye troubles returned. He could hardly read any more, and he had to put up with painful injections. It was some consolation when two American publishers offered him $11,000 in advance and 20 percent royalties on *Finnegans Wake*. But the novel was not to be completed for another decade.

Joyce left the education of their children mainly to Nora; he was occupied with other problems. Giorgio, who got along well with his father, made his debut as a singer in 1929. He married the divorced wife of an American friend, the former Mrs. Helen Kastor Fleischman. The birth of his grandchild, Stephen, inspired Joyce to write the poem "Ecce puer." Lucia's future was less promising. The frequent change of place may have been detrimental to her predisposition to schizophrenia. She had excellent training as a ballet dancer and took part in several performances. But in 1929 she began to feel that she was not physically strong enough for a dancing career and abandoned it. This seems to have been the beginning of her mental deterioration.

In 1929 the first book about "Work in Progress" came out; the title was ironic: *Our Exagmination round His Factification for Incamination of Work in Progress*. It consists of twelve essays, some of which had already been printed in *transition*. All the authors were friends of Joyce's, and it seems that the writing of the essays had been supervised by Joyce himself. He also supervised Stuart Gilbert's *James Joyce's Ulysses*, which appeared in 1930. At about this time he became acquainted with the Irish singer John Sullivan, a leading tenor of the Paris Opera. He was full of enthusiasm for the man and his voice; he started a propaganda crusade in order to procure engagements for him in England and America, where he had been neglected. Dr. Borsch, his eye specialist, died, and Joyce was advised to see the famous Swiss surgeon, Professor Alfred Vogt of Zurich, who had achieved extremely good results with his operations. In April 1930, Vogt successfully operated on one of Joyce's eyes.

Joyce thought it was high time that somebody should undertake the writing of his biography. He commissioned Herbert Gorman for the job. Richard Ellmann says that Joyce wished "to be treated as a saint with an unusually protracted martyrdom." [9] Gorman had the help of Stanislaus, Miss Beach, Miss Weaver, and others. Before the book was permitted to come out in 1939, Joyce changed some passages which he did not like; he added, changed, and distorted in a rather shameless manner. During the thirties he became more and more despotic: anybody who was not wholeheartedly for him was against him and was discarded. Sections of "Work in Progress" began to be published in limited editions by private presses. *Anna Livia Plurabelle* appeared in 1928, *Tales Told of Shem and Shaun* in 1929, and *Haveth Childers Everywhere* in 1930. All three booklets were reissued by T. S. Eliot's firm, Faber & Faber, between 1930 and 1932. The first of these episodes was translated into French by Samuel Beckett and Alfred Péron; their work was revised a first time by Paul Léon, Eugene Jolas, and Ivan Goll and a second time by Paul Léon, Philippe Soupault, and Joyce himself. The final text appeared in the *Nouvelle Revue Française* on May 1, 1931.

In the spring of 1931, Joyce, Nora, and Lucia went to London. They intended to settle in England permanently. For testamentary reasons, Joyce now married Nora legally. He had considerable capital— given to him by Miss Weaver. The interest from this and the regular royalties of *Ulysses* came to about $800 a month, at that time an enormous in-·come. In 1932, Joyce sold the American copyright for *Ulysses* (with Miss Beach's permission) to Random House, and B. W. Huebsch and the Viking Press obtained the preliminary rights for "Work in Progress." It was clear that *Ulysses* would be attacked for obscenity, but the publisher was optimistic and, in fact, won a memorable action against the New York Society for the Prevention of Vice.

On December 29, 1931, Joyce's father died. Of all his children, only James had remained in close and friendly contact with him; the others bore him a grudge for the misfortunes he had brought upon the family. He had hoped, in vain, that his favorite child would visit him and had made James Joyce his sole heir, out of gratitude for his affection. Joyce, who received a legacy of £665, had pangs of conscience. At the celebration of his fiftieth birthday (on February 2, 1932), Lucia threw a chair at Nora, and Giorgio took her to a mental hospital for a few days. Joyce's black mood improved on February 15, when Giorgio's son was born and was called Stephen James in honor of his grandfather and the hero of *A Portrait*. In order to spare his grandfather's feelings, the child was baptized secretly.

According to Richard Ellmann, it may have been Lucia's unrequited love for Samuel Beckett which hastened her mental deterioration. Beckett was a frequent visitor in Joyce's house, but he came to see Joyce, not his daughter, and he had no intention of marrying her. Nora thought that Lucia should be married off as soon as possible, that this would be the best guarantee for her mental health. Joyce's friend Paul Léon persuaded his brother-in-law to propose to Lucia. Giorgio intervened and said it would be an irresponsible action to want to attach Lucia to anybody. But Léon and Joyce thought otherwise. After the official engagement, Lucia broke down completely; it was confirmed that she was schizophrenic, and the engagement was forgotten. Her illness worsened rapidly; at the last moment, when the family was already sitting in the train, Lucia refused to go to London with them, and Joyce had to remain in Paris. She then refused to stay any longer with her parents and lived first in Léon's house and then with Mary and Padraic Colum. The psychiatrist had to visit her in disguise.

Meanwhile Joyce sold the European rights of *Ulysses;* the Odyssey Press brought out its first edition in 1932. Miss Beach was to receive 25 per cent of the royalties. The house of Faber & Faber was convinced that an English edition would be suppressed; John Lane finally took over *Ulysses*, and *Finnegans Wake* was to be published by Faber & Faber. Joyce's prestige had grown considerably during the 1920s. When an Academy of Irish Letters was founded in Ireland, Joyce was invited by Yeats to become a member, but he had to refuse, since an acceptance would have destroyed his public image as a martyr and an exile.

Although the doctors thought that Lucia should not live with her parents under any circumstances, Joyce decided to look after her himself. She was fond of her father but hated her mother. In the summer of 1932, Joyce went with her and Nora to Feldkirch, where he left Lucia with Eugene Jolas and his wife in order to return to Zurich to have his eyes examined. Professor Vogt postponed the operations because they were too dangerous at the moment. Maria Jolas suggested that they should have Lucia treated by C. G. Jung, but Joyce refused —Jung's negative article on *Ulysses* in mind—and sent her with a nurse to Vence on the Riviera while he established himself in Nice. He hoped that in this way she would feel independent although he was still nearby. But in October, Joyce, Nora, and Lucia were back in Paris. He gave Lucia 4000 francs to buy a fur coat. This, he prophesied, would get rid of her inferiority complex. The illness of his daughter was an enormous tragedy for Joyce and depressed him for the rest of his life. He could not accept the fact that her schizophrenia was incurable; he did not hesitate to dismiss anybody from his circle who dared to speak the truth. He trusted only those doctors who pretended to be optimistic. When their diagnoses became pessimistic, he took Lucia out of their care.

In May 1933, Joyce was back in Zurich with Lucia and Nora. If he did not want to go completely blind, an operation was now essential. Lucia had a new attack of hysteria, and Professor Hans W. Maier, director of the Mental Asylum of Burghölzli in Zurich, advised that she be taken to the clinic of Oscar Forel in Nyon. Joyce let her stay there for one week. In September the family was back in Paris, and Joyce corrected the proofs of Frank Budgen's book, *James Joyce and the Making of Ulysses*. Lucia now became quite ungovernable.

Twice she cut the telephone wires. On Joyce's fifty-second birthday she attacked Nora physically; Joyce sent her to Nyon again, where, this time, she stayed for several months. In the late summer of 1934, he visited her in Nyon. She was regressing both mentally and physically. She set her room on fire, after which Joyce took her to the Burghölzli clinic in Zurich.

Lucia had grown up in Zurich. It is one of the most awful insults among Zurich schoolchildren to say that the car from Burghölzli will come and get you. It is therefore quite understandable that Lucia wanted to go anywhere but there. Joyce understood her fears and transferred her to a clinic in Küsnacht where she came under C. G. Jung's personal care. He was Lucia's twentieth doctor, and, at the beginning, she seemed to like him. But Joyce had no sympathy for Jung's interpretation of her (and his) mental state. In January 1935, he took Lucia out of the clinic and got his sister Eileen to come and look after her. Lucia wanted to go to London with Eileen and stay with Miss Weaver. While Eileen visited Ireland, Lucia ran away, and Eileen had to return to London. This time, she took Lucia to Ireland with her, and Joyce reproached Miss Weaver for not having looked after his daughter. He contended that she was just as normal as he. Léon consoled Miss Weaver: "Mr. Joyce trusts one person alone, and this person is Lucia." [10] Lucia also ran away in Ireland. Three weeks after her return to Paris, in March 1936, she had to be carried out of the house in a strait jacket. From then on, she lived in clinics. Nevertheless, Joyce still believed in her eventual recovery, and nobody except Giorgio dared contradict him.

While the clouds of war were gathering on the horizon, Joyce drank even more than usual, and Nora often thought of leaving him. Their financial position was anything but satisfactory, despite the high income. The news came from Trieste that Stanislaus was to lose his position even though, this time, he had been careful to keep his political views to himself. In the late summer of 1936, Joyce traveled to Copenhagen, where he found to his great annoyance that Lawrence's *Lady Chatterley's Lover* was selling better than *Ulysses*. On his way back he visited Ernst Robert Curtius in Bonn to discuss "Work in Progress." In October 1936, Joyce met Stanislaus in Zurich. The latter was offered a position in the Institut Montana, which was on top of the Zugerberg and about an hour from Zurich. But he felt that the place was too lonely and returned to Trieste, where he finally obtained permission to continue in his position as Professor of English.

Although Joyce liked to read articles about himself, he tried to keep reporters and journalists away as much as possible. Very rarely did one of them succeed in meeting him. His circle of friends gradually grew smaller. Sullivan still belonged to it; so did Beckett, Paul Léon (who acted as secretary and looked after a large part of Joyce's correspondence), Stuart Gilbert, and Eugene and Maria Jolas. Joyce visited Lucia every week. In June 1937, he

addressed the P.E.N. Club in Paris. Although Joyce
was not interested in politics, he had no sympathy
for Hitler and the developments in Germany. He
refused, however, to write for the anti-Nazi periodical, *Mass und Wert*. On the other hand, he helped
several persons to escape from Germany and Austria, among them Hermann Broch, who had written
an important essay about Joyce (now in Vol. 1 of
Essays, Zurich, 1955). On November 13, 1938, *Finnegans Wake* was completed. The proof sheets
were read in a hurry and final corrections made.
The plan was to have the book published by February 2, Joyce's birthday. On January 30, the first
copy arrived from Faber & Faber. On May 4, 1939,
the novel appeared simultaneously in London and
New York. The reviews were not encouraging; few
critics pretended to understand the book, and by
some it was considered to be the product of a mad-
man, a bad joke. Oliver Gogarty called it "the most
colossal leg pull in literature since Macpherson's
Ossian."[11] But there were at least two excellent reviews by important critics: those of Harry Levin
and Edmund Wilson.

There are several accesses to *Finnegans Wake*.
The easiest one today is, no doubt, Anthony Burgess' introduction ("What It's All About") to his
edition of *A Shorter Finnegans Wake*. He prints
about a third of the original work, interrupting
Joyce's text here and there with explanatory passages which are to keep the reader on the right
track. Some Joyceans still swear by Campbell and
Robinson's *A Skeleton Key to Finnegans Wake*,

which has helped the uninitiated since 1944. It contains a nine-page synopsis followed by a running commentary of more than 300 pages. *Finnegans Wake* consists of four parts which Campbell and Robinson call "The Book of Parents," "The Book of the Sons," "The Book of the People," and "Recorso." Joyce did not use titles or numbers to designate these four parts or the chapters, and there is no agreement among critics on how to name the books or the chapters. (The first book has eight chapters, the next two have four each, and the last book consists of one chapter.) Another synopsis can be found in William York Tindall's *A Reader's Guide to James Joyce* (pp. 265–296). He calls the four parts "The Fall of Man," "Conflict," "Humanity," and "Renewal." Hardly any theory influenced Joyce so much as Vico's teaching that world history continually repeats itself and does so in four stages: theocracy is followed by aristocracy, this by democracy, and democracy leads to chaos. The last stage is characterized by an excessive individualism and ends in destruction. Through a world catastrophe humanity is once more made aware of the supernatural, and the cycle begins again with theocracy. Tindall very convincingly assigns each book and each chapter to one of Vico's "ages": the divine age, the heroic age, the human age, and the recorso. The title *Finnegans Wake* suggests that Joyce had Vico, among other people, in mind when composing his book. "Finnegan" can be spelled as "Fin" (the end) and "again." The first half of the first sentence of the book can be found at the end of the last page,

pointing to the fact that the book has no beginning
and no end. To make quite sure that the reader
would understand this, Joyce used the article "the"
as the last word in the book, one of the few words
that can never stand at the end of a sentence. It be-
longs to the noun "riverrun," the first word in the
novel. A further synopsis is contained in Adaline
Glasheen's *A Second Census of Finnegans Wake*
(pp. xxiii–lix). It is followed by a most useful list of
"Who is Who When Everybody Is Somebody
Else," in which she enumerates all the transformations in which the main persons of *Finnegans Wake*
appear.

There is no agreement about the exact contents of *Finnegans Wake*. Every synopsis seems to
refer to a different book. How helpful, really, is a
summing-up of the contents of *Finnegans Wake*? It
would be just as useful to give a summing-up of a
telephone directory or of a country's official train
schedule. The general outline counts for little; all
the important information is to be found in the details. There is, of course, some kind of structure: the
telephone book is organized alphabetically, the train
directory according to the time span of one day;
Finnegans Wake is parallel to Vico's cycle and the
eternal repetition of fall and rise. Everybody in the
book falls and rises: Finnegan falls off the ladder
and rises at the wake; political leaders like Parnell
and Caesar rise and fall, so do Adam, Earwicker,
Christ, Anna Livia Plurabelle, the sun, water, and
the penis. This falling and rising repeats itself in
eternal circles: the sun; the moon; the movement of

water from the land to the sea and back—as clouds
and rain—to the land; the rising of life from the dust;
and its return to dust; and the course of history
through Vico's four ages.

Another access to *Finnegans Wake* is the early
manuscripts, especially David Hayman's *A First-
Draft Version of Finnegans Wake*. This is less than
half as long as the final version, and the words are
spelled in a much more conventional way than in
later versions. By reproducing the manuscripts with
all the additions and corrections, Hayman has given
the reader a good insight into Joyce's method of construction. But the first-draft version will only help
with the elucidation of some words, sentences, or
shorter passages, not with the book as a whole. The
overall contents remain just as obscure as in the
final version. The synopses by Tindall, Glasheen,
or Campbell and Robinson read like surrealist tales
by Arp, but they lack Arp's humor. This is not
Joyce's fault, of course, because *Finnegans Wake*
contains, on the average, more humor per page than
most books in world literature. This fact is the most
important one to keep in mind when starting to read
the *Wake*. As Anthony Burgess said: "Before we
start reading we ought to put off the mask of solem-
nity and prepare to be entertained. This is one of
the most entertaining books ever written." [12]

Burgess, like everybody else before him, tries
to explain *Finnegans Wake* as a book of dreams.
Nobody is quite sure who dreams: H. C. Earwicker, his wife, a giant, Joyce himself, or several
persons including or excluding any of these four?

Why should this be a dream book? Because Joyce has said so himself. *Ulysses* was a "day" book, *Finnegans Wake* a "night" book. Everybody has gratefully accepted this explanation; in dreams, they say, everything turns into everything else, and the most impossible things take place, just as in *Finnegans Wake.* They forget one fact: dreams are usually quite clear. Joyce had dreams and told them to his friends in perfectly reasonable English. If you want to know how extraordinarily clear a dream-landscape is, put a record player under your bed, and choose a record of quiet piano music. Install an extension cable into a friend's room, and at three o'clock in the morning when you are deeply asleep, have your friend plug in the cable. The music will slowly build itself into the dream you are having at the moment and eventually wake you up in such a way that you will, in most cases, remember the last portion of your dream. Write it down immediately. There will be no ambiguity whatever in your language, although some of your dreams will make no sense to you at all, and much of it will be devoid of normal daytime logic. Kafka, with his extraordinarily precise language, wrote the dream books of our time. His tales have the logic and quality of dreams—but not *Finnegans Wake.* Joyceans will probably counter by arguing that Joyce wanted to describe the dreams of the collective unconscious, of archetypes. But there is nothing in *Finnegans Wake* to warrant any such explanation. The details can all be explained at the level of consciousness; to understand *Finnegans Wake,* linguistics is the helpful discipline, not psychology. If much of *Finnegans Wake* makes no sense, then it is for one obvious reason: Joyce changed the spelling too much. Often we could refer to earlier versions and find the doubtful word or sentence in a less distorted shape and so get at the original meaning. But what for? The quality does not lie in the original sentence, but in the associations of the distorted one.

Joyce did not expect us to search around for any basic meaning. Certainly he was a very arrogant person, an egoist *in extremis*, and he is supposed to have said that he expected his readers to spend a lifetime on *Finnegans Wake*. Maybe one should spend a lifetime on it—but not by trying to attach a basic meaning to every word or sentence. This would miss Joyce's purpose entirely. Few people will want to read more than a few pages at one sitting because the fun in reading allusively misspelt words pales after a while. But you can go back to the book the next week and continue, and when you arrive at the last page, begin again; this time you will discover more allusions than during the previous reading. Solving a crossword puzzle every day provides a similar satisfaction, except that with Joyce, if you have the right kind of humor and sensitivity, you also get a good many laughs.

Finnegans Wake is not for everybody, and it is ironical that it is often the wrong kind of reader who has a go at it, writes about it, and by his writing frightens off the right kind of reader. Burgess says: "Joyce scholarship has become a major industry in some American universities, but in Great Britain it

has hardly as yet come into existence." [13] Why?
American universities, compared to English ones,
turn out immense numbers of graduates with doc-
toral degrees. If a professor of English has a student who has difficulties organizing his thoughts, he
will give him a thesis topic which he hopes will give
the student no chance to get into wild speculations
—a topic such as the "Chinese Elements in *Finnegans
Wake*." Books about Joyce have a good market, and
a good many such theses are published. They are
enthusiastically received by Joyceans since they will
contain a few new "splendid identifications" (Glasheen), for example, explanations of allusions in misspelt words. Non-Joyceans who have written their
theses on more demanding topics will frown upon
such crossword puzzlers and not take them seriously. It is significant that many Joyce scholars will
deal exclusively with Joyce for the rest of their lives
because they would be unable to write intelligently
on any other subject. *Finnegans Wake* scholarship
usually means one thing only: to list more and more
identifications until every word in the book is logically accounted for. These Joyce scholars—most of
whom demonstrate an appalling lack of humor—
have, of course, the privilege to write and publish
their work, and it is not their fault if their efforts are
taken too seriously and if many people conclude
that *FinnegansWake* must be the most boring book
in world literature.

Still, *Finnegans Wake* is not for everybody to
read. If you do not know German, Italian, and
French, you will miss at least half the fun. You

must be prepared for the fact that Joyce was obsessed by cloacal matters. In sixteenth- and seven-
teenth-century Germany, any reference to farting,
shitting, pissing, or sexual contact was considered
hilarious in itself. Joyce had the same mentality. His
Swiss friend August Suter said that Joyce savored
obscene words like candy. Furthermore, *Finnegans
Wake* makes fun of everything: the more taboo the
objects ridiculed, the greater the shock (or the
amusement) of the reader. Joyce blasphemes and
blasts away with increased intensity against the
Catholic Church. Jesus is reviled, Holy Mary is put
with the whores, Joseph is a cuckold, the Holy
Ghost an adulterer, the participants at communion
cannibals, and so on. Among other things, *Finnegans Wake* is a black mass in linguistics; but the
Devil gets his share as does everybody else.

If we read Hans Arp and Vicente Huidobro's
surrealistic tales in *Drei und drei surreale Geschich-
ten* (Berlin, 1963, written in 1931), we shall have to
laugh at every sentence. We understand all the
words, the sentences are grammatically correct, but
the meaning is nonsensical. Like Joyce, Arp and
Huidobro took their products extremely seriously.
In his introduction to the book, Huidobro says that
this kind of laughing is as much a psychological
safety valve as is crying. *Finnegans Wake* is a surrealistic work. Joyce went further than Arp. Joyce
broke with conventional grammar if he thought the
sound and rhythm warranted it, and he misspelled
words in such a way that the reader could either
discover several meanings in them ("penisolate") or

at least laugh about their spelling ("toilet" for "to let"). While Arp wrote according to the law of chance and accident ("Gesetz des Zufalls"), Joyce arrived at his surrealism in an indirect way—by multiplying meanings; hence the chronologically more and more obscure versions of *Finnegans Wake*. But the "Gesetz des Zufalls" played a very large part in his composition too.

When reading *Finnegans Wake* for the first time, some impatient people may find it useful to have Adaline Glasheen's "Who is Who" at hand (pp. lx-lxvi). Five individuals and one group of persons appear again and again, under different names and shapes and at different times in world history. There is Mr. Porter, who keeps a pub in Chapelizod, on the other side of Phoenix Park in Dublin. He has a dark spot in his past—something about girls in the park—and is called Humphrey Chimpden Earwicker. Why? It has been explained that he has an unconscious wish to commit incest with his daughter but does not admit this thought to his conscious mind. Therefore, every time the word "incest" comes up, he spells it as "insect." Hence he is an insect—but not in actual fact, like Gregor Samsa in Kafka's "The Metamorphosis"—only in name; earwig is an insect. Earwig in French is "perce-oreille," and this sounds like Persse O'Reilly—another name for Earwicker. The initials H. C. E. reappear in hundreds of three-word groups throughout the book. Earwicker is also God, Adam, Abraham, Lot, Tim Finnegan, and about fifty other figures, among them James Joyce himself. Earwicker's wife,

Anna Livia Plurabelle, is his feminine equivalent, Nora, the river Liffey, the mother of God, and so on. Her daughter, Issy, stands for any aspect of a young and pretty woman: Eve, Ophelia, Juliet, Isolde, and Cleopatra. The twins Shem and Shaun are often fighting—as were Abel and Cain, St. Michael and Lucifer, James Joyce and Stanislaus, and Mulligan and Stephen Dedalus. Shem seems to be the artist type, Shaun the man of the world. The rest of the personnel consists mostly of groups of four (the Evangelists, the four Elders) or twelve (the Apostles). To be given any additional information in advance might do more harm than good. Who knows which of the several synopses contains the most truth —if any? It could spoil the fun of reading *Finnegans Wake* if the reader were to look for situations and happenings which are enumerated in a synopsis and then not be able to find them because a critic, unable to make head or tail of a passage, had gotten his information from another critic or from a letter of Joyce's about an earlier (and different) version of the passage under analysis. It is better and safer to enjoy the word play and the associations with an unprejudiced mind.

Finnegans Wake, then, is a book of laughter. Some Joyceans would never admit this because they believe that this would reduce the stature of the work. Why should it? It is a unique book. There are no literary clichés on its 628 pages. It can be enjoyed if read aloud (rhythm, sound) or if read in silence (word plays, spelling). It has no message; it is not a tragedy, not a drama; it contains lyrical poetry and

elements of comedy; it is a huge collection of puns, a
parody of every art and science, a parody of language and of civilization. Some critics have been put
off by Joyce's method of construction. He would
write a sentence, then look at each word carefully.
Could it not be transformed in such a way that it
would become ambiguous—so that each of several
possible meanings suggested by the uncommon
spelling would refer to other words or happenings
in the book? Children take great pleasure in transforming words, but they are extremely offended if
it is done with their names. Joyce had preserved
this pleasure. People pay off old scores by calling
each other names. There is no doubt that, as in his
previous books, Joyce is settling many scores in *Finnegans Wake*. By twisting his "friends'" names and
by putting them among suggestive words, he felt he
was taking his revenge—and it made him feel better.
Even after the publication in 1939, Joyce continued
to distort and add. The later corrections were at
first published separately, but since 1958 they have
been incorporated into the text.

This is, of course, a strange way to go about
constructing a piece of literature, and it does sound
stupid if a critic goes and lists all the various spell-
ings of Copenhagen:

Cokenhape,	Capeinhope,	Culpenhelp,	Wolkencap,
Wapentake,	holpenstake,	Cupenhave,	Copemanhelpen,
kokkenhovens,	Coxenhagen,	Cabinhogan,	help of me cope
hopenhaven, etc.[14]			

This is exactly what one should not do. It is as intelligent as lining up all verses in Goethe's poetry

which contain the rhyme "Herz-Schmerz." Critics may question the use of putting a few hundred names of rivers into a chapter. When asked why he did it, Joyce told Max Eastman that perhaps one day a child in Somaliland or Tibet would read the book and be pleased to find a river in his own country mentioned. It throws an interesting light on those Joyceans who accept this explanation with an approving nod.

Finnegans Wake was never meant to be "understood" in the way the plot of a traditional novel should be understood. In any case, that would be impossible. Joyce told Nino Frank to translate (with his help) the Anna Livia Plurabelle chapter into Italian: "We must do the job now before it is too late; for the moment there is at least one person, myself, who can understand what I am writing. I don't however guarantee that in two or three years I'll still be able to." [15] Joyce was the only one who ever knew *all* the reasons why a word was in a certain place and spelled in a certain way. Can *Finnegans Wake* be translated? It has been done: parts of the novel have appeared in several languages; Joyce himself helped with the French and Italian fragments. But, fundamentally, *Finnegans Wake* exists because English spelling differs so much from pronunciation; or better, you can spell any sound in any number of ways. German, French, and Italian have fewer possibilities. Also, the art of punning is, in line with the nature of the language, an English art. It is much less common in other European languages. And then, too, nobody can be sure of all the original meanings of *Finnegans Wake*. How do we translate "penisolate" into German? Which German word contains "Isolde," "Feder," "Penis," and "Halbinsel"? The fragments that have been published from the planned German translation of *Finnegans Wake* sound and look like the world record in literary inanity. It would be more intelligent to pay the salary of a skilled linguist (with a sense of humor), tell him to study Joyce's methods, and then go to work on, say, *Faust or Zauberberg*. After seventeen years he might have produced something that would beat Joyce by several miles!

When war broke out Joyce had just returned from Switzerland and was staying in La Baule. Dr. Delmas, the director of the mental hospital in Paris where Lucia was staying, was planning to have his patients and staff transported to Brittany. Joyce was afraid that Paris would be bombed and tried to have Lucia come to La Baule at once. But there were no more private cars, and Lucia arrived with Delmas' other patients in the middle of September. Meanwhile Giorgio's marriage broke up; his wife suffered one nervous breakdown after another and had to be hospitalized. Joyce's friend, Paul Léon, blamed Giorgio for his wife's mental state. Joyce was not of the same opinion, and Paul Léon was expelled from his circle of friends. Joyce was drinking more than ever. When he and Nora arrived in Saint-Gérand-le-Puy on the day before Christmas, 1939, he was seized with violent cramps in the stomach. Joyce thought it was nerves and refused to see a doctor. It seems that this was the first indication of the duodenal ulcer which brought about his death a year later.

Saint-Gérand-le-Puy is a small community near Vichy. Maria Jolas had transferred her École Bilingue from Paris to this place, which was expected to be safe from bombs. Joyce and Nora were soon bored stiff in their new rural environment. He read Goethe's conversation with Eckermann, told his grandson Stephen stories about *Ulysses*, and was once more working on *Finnegans Wake*, concocting and twisting words and changing the punctuation. In early April, he and Nora moved to Vichy for two months. In May, the German army entered France and was in Paris on June 14. Beckett arrived in Saint-Gérand-le-Puy without a penny, followed by Giorgio; Helen had been taken back to America by her brother just in time. Léon turned up, and Joyce was reconciled with him. The Germans occupied Saint-Gérand-le-Puy for a few days but withdrew after a new French government in Vichy had been established. Joyce continued drinking, and his health grew worse.

Life could not continue in this way for long. Léon returned to Paris and handed over Joyce's papers and effects to the Irish consul. In 1941, Léon was arrested by the Nazis and killed the next year. Maria Jolas set out to America to join her husband; Joyce refused to go with her. He applied to the Swiss consulate in Lyons for permission to stay in Switzerland for the duration of the war. Switzerland was crowded with refugees. The hotels in tourist centers were full of them. The little neutral country was completely surrounded by the Germans and Italians; it had no access to the sea. Switzerland could not produce enough food even for its own population. Its very existence depended on the good will of Germany and Italy. All imports had to pass through Nazi territory. No wonder the Swiss were reluctant to add to the large number of refugees they already had to feed. And, after all, there was no reason why Joyce, being Irish, could not apply for Irish passports and go back to his native country, which was neutral too. However, Joyce did not want to abandon his martyrdom and be grateful to Ireland for anything. He knew how to apply to the right people and some members of the intellectual and political elite in Zurich were willing enough to help him into the country. Alfred Vogt, Othmar Schoeck, Robert Faesi, Theodor Spörri, Ernst Howald, Heinrich Straumann, even the mayor himself spoke up for him, and finally permission to reside in Zurich was granted. Sigfried Giedion and Edmund Brauchbar had to pay a security of 20,000 Swiss francs. On November 29, the Swiss embassy in Vichy received orders to make out the visa. On December 14, 1940, Joyce, Nora, Giorgio, and Stephen arrived in Geneva. On the following day they were in Lausanne, and on December 17 the family arrived in Zurich.

The Joyces took rooms in the Pension Delphin which was in the same part of town where they had lived during the First World War. Joyce lived in seclusion and received few visitors. On January 10, Joyce and some friends celebrated Paul Ruggiero's birthday in the restaurant Kronenhalle, where Joyce was a regular guest. Back home he collapsed with violent stomach pains. At two o'clock Giorgio called a doctor. In the morning Joyce was taken to the hospital to have an x-ray. His ulcer had perforated, and an immediate operation was necessary. It was considered successful, and by the afternoon everything seemed to be in order. But the next morning Joyce became weaker; he died in the early morning of January 13, 1941. The funeral took place two days later at the Fluntern cemetery. The English ambassador in Switzerland, the Swiss poet Max Geilinger, and Heinrich Straumann gave the addresses. Nora chose to stay in Zurich, where she died ten years later. Stanislaus died in 1955, Eva in 1957, and Eileen in 1963. Joyce's daughter Lucia went to live in an English hospital, and his son Giorgio settled in Munich.

There is no doubt that Joyce has played an important part in the development of the twentieth-century novel. His influence on other writers cannot be overrated. It is always a certain aspect of a work of literature which has an influence—and this influence is often based on a misunderstanding. In the case of *Ulysses*, it is to be found in the technique of the interior monologue, which, so Joyce says, he took over from Dujardin. Arthur Schnitzler had already used the technique before Joyce, but only after *Ulysses* did it become a common literary device. Joyce's whole literary unconventionality had a very strong effect: his work encouraged writers to experiment more and more freely. This does not mean that Joyce's influence was necessarily all for the best. One might ask: Did not the so-called "decadence of the novel" begin with Joyce? Conrad felt the demonic evil of his time but was satisfied in portraying it objectively. Lawrence, on the other hand, warned and fought; he was the prophet with a solution. Joyce took pleasure in destroying in advance what would have collapsed anyway. Destruction and decadence, as he knew from Vico, are necessary steps in the course of things. Joyce was the one who advanced furthest and most boldly toward the abolition of the kind of literature and art which humanity has known since the time of Aristotle. It would be difficult to imagine a work of literature on the other side of *Finnegans Wake.* Sometime, maybe, an author will find that only by writing in a new alphabet can he do justice to his thoughts and feelings, or he will throw away his pen and sell his works in the form of x-ray films of his brain at work. Then, of course, *Finnegans Wake* will look quite old-fashioned. In the meantime, Joyce's works will be on the shelves of anybody interested in modern literature; his first books will be read with pleasure, *Ulysses* and *Finnegans Wake* either with laughter or with antlike industry; all are essential documents of the literature of our time.

Chronology

1882: James Joyce was born on February 2, in Dublin.

1888: He entered Clongowes Wood College in September.

1893: He continued his schooling at Belvedere College.

1899–1902: He studied at University College.

1900: Joyce's review of Ibsen's *When We Dead Awaken* was published in the London *Fortnightly Review* in April.

1902–1903: He made his first two trips to Paris.

1904: He met Nora Barnacle and traveled with her to Pola (Yugoslavia) where he taught English at the Berlitz school.

1905: He was transferred to the Berlitz school in Trieste. His son Giorgio was born.

1907: His daughter Lucia Anna was born in Trieste.

1912: Joyce made his last trip to Ireland.

1914: *Dubliners* was published in London. *A Portrait of the Artist as a Young Man* was serialized in the *Egoist* (February 2, 1914 to September 1, 1915).

1915–1919: Joyce spent the war in Zurich.

1916: *A Portrait* was published in New York.

1917: *A Portrait* was published in London.

1918: *Exiles* was published. *The Little Review* (New York) began serialization of *Ulysses*.

1919: Joyce returned to Trieste.

1920: He arrived in Paris where he remained until 1940.

1922: *Ulysses* was published in Paris.

1934: *Ulysses* was published in New York.

1939: *Finnegans Wake* was published in England and America.

1940: After a stay in St. Gérand-le-Puy near Vichy, Joyce was given permission to enter Switzerland.

1941: James Joyce died on January 13, in Zurich, as a result of a perforated ulcer.

Notes

Chapter 1

1 Scholes, Robert, and Richard M. Kain. *The Workshop of Daedalus*, 1965, p. 270.
2 *Ibid.*, p. 280.
3 O'Connor, Ulick, Ed., *The Joyce We Knew*, 1967, p. 15.
4 *Letters of James Joyce.* Vol. I, 1957, Stuart Gilbert, Ed.; Vols. II and III, 1966, Richard Ellmann, Ed. (Hereafter referred to as *Letters*.) Vol. II, p. 48.
5 *Letters*, Vol. II, p. 124.
6 *Letters*, Vol. I, p. 52.
7 Joyce, James. *Stephen Hero*, 1944, p. 211.
8 Gogarty as quoted in Scholes and Kain, p. 7.
9 The epiphany as printed in Scholes and Kain, p. 26.
10 Ellmann, Richard. *James Joyce*, 1966, p. 113.
11 *Loc. cit.*

Chapter 2

1 *Letters of James Joyce.* Vol. I, 1957, Stuart Gilbert, Ed.;
   Vols. II and III, 1966, Richard Ellmann, Ed. (Hereafter
   referred to as *Letters.*) Vol. II, p. 182.
2 Ellmann, Richard. *James Joyce,* 1966, p. 270.
3 Joyce, James. *Dubliners,* Compass Books, 1967, p. 132.
4 *Letters,* Vol. II, p. 134.
5 *Ibid.,* p. 99.
6 *Ibid.,* p. 217.
7 Ellmann, *James Joyce,* p. 353.
8 Joyce, James. *Giacomo Joyce,* "Introduction" by Richard
   Ellmann, 1968, p. ix.
9 *Ibid.,* p. xvii.
10 Joyce, James. *A Portrait of the Artist as a Young Man,*
   Compass Books, 1964, p. 171.
11 *Letters,* Vol. II, p. 255.
12 Joyce, *A Portrait,* p. 240.
13 *Ibid.,* p. 247.

Chapter 3

1 *Letters of James Joyce.* Vol. I, 1957, Stuart Gilbert, Ed.;
   Vols. II and III, 1966, Richard Ellmann, Ed. (Hereafter
   referred to as *Letters.*) Vol. III, p. 22.
2 Joyce, James. *Exiles,* London: The New English Library,
   Four Square Edition, 1962, p. 8.
3 *Ibid.,* p. 157.
4 *Ibid.,* p. 86.
5 *Ibid.,* p. 87.
6 *Ibid.,* p. 113.

Chapter 4

1 Ellmann, Richard. *James Joyce*, 1966, p. 527.
2 Gilbert, Stuart. *James Joyce's Ulysses*, 1963, p. 38.
3 Tindall, William York. *A Reader's Guide to James Joyce*, 1959, p. 123.
4 Joyce, James. *Ulysses*, London, 1960, p. 107.
5 Budgen, Frank. *James Joyce and the Making of Ulysses*, 1960, pp. 122–23.
6 Tindall, p. 185.
7 Joyce, *Ulysses*, pp. 328–29.
8 Greenway, John. "A Guide through James Joyce's *Ulysses*," *College English*, Nov. 1955, p. 74.
9 *Letters of James Joyce*. Vol. I, 1957, Stuart Gilbert, Ed.; Vols. II and III, 1966, Richard Ellmann, Ed. (Hereafter referred to as *Letters*.) Vol. III, p. 103.
10 Senn, Fritz. "Zum Gespräch über Joyce," *Neue Zürcher Zeitung*, March 14, 1964.
11 *Letters*, Vol. III, p. 103.
12 As quoted from *Dial* in Ellmann, *James Joyce*, p. 541.
13 *Letters*, Vol. III, p. 58.

Chapter 5

1 *Letters of James Joyce*. Vol. I, 1957, Stuart Gilbert, Ed., Vols. II and III, 1966, Richard Ellmann, Ed. (Hereafter referred to as *Letters*.) Vol. III, p. 103.
2 *Loc. cit.*
3 Harriet Weaver's letter as quoted in Richard Ellmann, *James Joyce*, 1966, p. 594.
4 *Letters*, Vol. I, pp. 247–48.
5 *Loc. cit.*
6 Harriet Weaver's letter as quoted in Ellmann, *James Joyce*, p. 596.
7 *Letters*, Vol. III, p. 145.

[8] Joyce, James. *Finnegans Wake*, Compass Books, 1959, p. 3.

[9] Ellmann, *James Joyce*, p. 644.

[10] *Ibid.*, p. 695.

[11] Gogarty's review in the *Observer* (May 7, 1939) as quoted in Ellmann, *James Joyce*, p. 734.

[12] Burgess, Anthony. *A Shorter Finnegans Wake*, 1966, p. 6.

[13] *Loc. cit.*

[14] Boldereff, F. M. *Reading Finnegans Wake*, 1959. See the Idioglossary.

[15] As quoted in Ellmann, *James Joyce*, p. 713.

Selected Bibliography

I   The Best Editions of Joyce's Works

Dubliners. Text corrected by Robert Scholes, Viking Press (Compass), 1967.

A Portrait of the Artist as a Young Man. Text corrected by Chester G. Anderson, Viking Press (Compass), 1964 and after.

Exiles. Editions since 1951 contain Joyce's notes on the play.

Ulysses. In U.S.A.: Modern Library (editions since 1961); in England: The Bodley Head (editions since 1960); in Europe: The Odyssey Press (editions since 1933).

Finnegans Wake (with the author's corrections incorporated in the text). Viking Press (Compass), 1959 and after.

Stephen Hero (augmented text). New Directions, 1963.

The Critical Writings of James Joyce. Edited by Ellsworth Mason and Richard Ellmann, Viking Press, 1959.

Collected Poems. Viking Press (Compass), 1957.

Letters of James Joyce. Vol. I edited by Stuart Gilbert, Viking Press, 1957; Vols. II and III edited by Richard Ellmann, Viking Press, 1966.

Giacomo Joyce. Edited by Richard Ellmann, Viking Press, 1968.

II Bibliography and Critical Reputation

Magalaner, Marvin, and Richard M. Kain. *Joyce, the Man, the Work, the Reputation,* 1956 (paperback, 1962).

Modern Fiction Studies, Vol. 4 (Spring 1958). Contains a checklist of Joyce criticism.

Parker, Alan. *James Joyce: A Bibliography of His Writings, Critical Material, and Miscellanea,* 1948.

Slocum, John, and Herbert Cahoon. *A Bibliography of James Joyce,* 1953.

III Biographies

Anderson, Chester G. *James Joyce and His World* (124 illustrations), 1967.

Ellmann, Richard. *James Joyce,* 1959 (paperback, 1966).

Gorman, Herbert. *James Joyce* (new edition), 1949.

IV   Short General Introductions

Burgess, Anthony. *Re Joyce*, 1965 (paperback, 1968).
Levin, Harry. *James Joyce* (augmented edition), 1960.
Tindall, William York. *A Reader's Guide to James Joyce*, 1959.

V   Interpretations of Joyce's Main Works

A   *Dubliners*

Gifford, Don: *Notes for Joyce*, 1967. A list of allusions in *Dubliners* and *A Portrait*.
Moynihan, William T., Ed. *Joyce's "The Dead,"* 1965. Contains essays on the early work by several hands.

B   *A Portrait of the Artist as a Young Man*

Connolly, Thomas E., Ed. *Joyce's "Portrait": Criticisms and Critiques*, 1962.
Ryf, Robert S. *A New Approach to Joyce: The Portrait of the Artist as a Guidebook*, 1961 (paperback, 1964).
Scholes, Robert, and Richard M. Kain, Eds. *The Workshop of Daedalus*, 1965. Contains all epiphanies, material from notebooks, biographical background material, and extracts from books which influenced Joyce.

C   *Ulysses*

Adams, Robert Martin. *Surface and Symbol: The Consistency of James Joyce's Ulysses*, 1962 (paperback, 1967).

Blamires, Harry. *The Bloomsday Book: A Guide through Joyce's Ulysses*, 1966.

Budgen, Frank. *James Joyce and the Making of Ulysses* (new edition), 1960.

Flora, Francesco. *Poesia e Impoesia nell' Ulisse di Joyce*, Milan: 1962.

Gilbert, Stuart. *James Joyce's Ulysses* (revised edition), 1952.

Goldberg, S. L. *The Classical Temper: A Study of James Joyce's Ulysses*, 1961.

Greenway, John. "A Guide through James Joyce's *Ulysses*," *College English* (Nov. 1955), pp. 67–78.

Hanley, Miles. *Word Index to James Joyce's Ulysses*, 1951.

Kain, Richard M. *Fabulous Voyager: James Joyce's Ulysses* (revised edition), 1959.

Litz, A. Walton. *The Art of James Joyce: Method and Design in Ulysses and Finnegans Wake* (augmented edition), 1964.

Prescott, Joseph. *Exploring James Joyce*, 1964.

Smith, Paul Jordan. *A Key to the Ulysses of James Joyce*, 1927 and after.

Sultan, Stanley. *The Argument of Ulysses*, 1964.

Thornton, Weldon. *Allusions in Ulysses*, 1968.

D   *Finnegans Wake*

Beckett, Samuel, and others: *Our Exagmination Round His Factification for Incamination of Work in Progress* (new edition), 1961.

Benstock, Bernard. *Joyce—Again's Wake: An Analysis of Finnegans Wake*, 1965.

Bonheim, Helmut. *A Lexicon of the German in Finnegans Wake*, 1967.

Burgess, Anthony, Ed. *A Shorter Finnegans Wake*, 1966.

Campbell, Joseph, and Henry Morton Robinson. *A Skeleton Key to Finnegans Wake* (new edition), 1961.

Christiani, Donina Bunis. *Scandinavian Elements of Finnegans Wake*, 1965.

Connolly, Thomas E. *James Joyce's Scribbledehobble; The Ur-Workbook for Finnegans Wake*, 1961.

Dalton, Jack P., and Clive Heart, Eds. *Twelve and a Tilly: Essays on the Occasion of the 25th Anniversary of Finnegans Wake*, 1966.

Glasheen, Adaline. *A Second Census of Finnegans Wake: An Index of the Characters and Their Roles*, 1963.

Hayman, David, Ed. *A First-Draft Version of Finnegans Wake*, 1963.

Heart, Clive. *A Concordance to Finnegans Wake*, 1963.

———. *Structure and Motif in Finnegans Wake*, 1962.

Higginson, Fred H. *Anna Livia Plurabelle: The Making of a Chapter*, 1960.

VI Other Biographical Works of Special Interest

Byrne, J. F. *Silent Years*, 1953.

Colum, Mary and Padraic. *Our Friend James Joyce*, 1958.

Curran, C. P. *James Joyce Remembered*, 1968.

Healey, George Harris, Ed. *The Dublin Diary of Stanislaus Joyce*, 1962.

Hutchins, Patricia. *James Joyce's Dublin*, 1950.

———. *James Joyce's World*, 1957.

Joyce, Stanislaus. *My Brother's Keeper*, 1958.

O'Connor, Ulick. *The Joyce We Knew*, Cork, 1967. Memoirs by Eugene Sheehy, William G. Fallon, Padraic Colum, and Arthur Power.

Pinguentini, Gianni. *James Joyce in Italia*, Verona, 1963.

Read, Forrest, Ed. *Pound/Joyce: Letters and Essays*, 1968.

VII Critical Works of Special Interest

Atherton, James S. *The Books at the Wake*, 1960.

Givens, Seon, Ed. *James Joyce: Two Decades of Criticism*, 1948. Contains essays by James T. Farrell, T. S. Eliot, Edmund Wilson, and others.

Hodgart, Matthew J. C., and Mabel P. Worthington. *Song in the Works of James Joyce*, 1959.

Magalaner, Marvin, Ed. *A James Joyce Miscellany*, 1957. Contains essays by Thornton Wilder, Alfred Kerr, and others.

————. *A James Joyce Miscellany* (second series,) 1959.

————. *A James Joyce Miscellany* (third series), 1962.

Moseley, Virginia. *Joyce and the Bible*, 1957.

Noon, William T. *Joyce and Aquinas*, 1957.

O'Brien, Darcy. *The Conscience of James Joyce*, 1968.

Schutte, William. *Joyce and Shakespeare*, 1957.

Tysdahl, B. J. *Joyce and Ibsen*, 1968.